The 2020's

Billions will
create/consume/connect
from their pocket

AKcidentalwriter

ISBN 978-1-7376149-0-6 (paperback)
ISBN 978-1-7376149-1-3 (eBook)

Copyright © 2021 by AKcidentalwriter

All rights reserved. No part of this publication may be reproduced, distributed, or transmitted in any form or by any means, including photocopying, recording, or other electronic or mechanical methods without the prior written permission of the publisher.

Printed in the United States of America

CONTENTS

Part 1 1
Segment 0 – The Ultimate Reality 7
Segment 1 – Only Caterer in Town 9
Segment 2 – You do not have to wait..11
Segment 3 – The Age of the unprofessional..12
Segment 4 – Data and Advertising Racket..14
Segment 5 – Reach Versus Engagement...16
Segment 6 – Discovery vs. A Hit 18
Segment 7 – The Push and Pull 20
Segment 8 – 15 Second racket 22
Segment 9 – Famedom versus Stardom 24
Segment 10 – Social Capital 25
Segment 11 – The death of Editorial 27
Segment 12 – Traditional advertising 2020 29
Segment 13 – Future is fragmented and miniature during 2020's 30
Segment 14 – Future comes fast 32
Segment 15 – Equity of Experiences...34
Segment 16 – Why songs will be important in 2020's 36
Segment 17 – The wrap up 37

Part 2: The 2020'S 39
Digital Relevance Can't be Bought but it can be Manipulated.....................................41
Introduction..45
Chapter 0 – Connection Economy 47
Chapter 1 – The Mystique is Gone..49
Chapter 2 – Karaokezation of Music 51
Chapter 3 – Cut Out The Unnecessary Middleman 53
Chapter 4 – Breaking A Song vs Breaking A Artist 54
Chapter 5 – References and Relationships 56
Chapter 6 – Music As A Branding Tool..59
Chapter 7 – PR Has Been Replaced By Social Media Trolling....................................61
Chapter 8 – Mainstream is Dead in 2017...63
Chapter 9 – The Global Record 65
Chapter 10 – The Store Don't Close 66
Chapter 11 – The Store Is In Your Pocket 67
Epilogue..71

- Part 3: Post Covid-19 75
  - Digital Bill of Rights 79
  - Forewarned 81
  - Observation 1 – The human is a biohazard in the 2020 P.C (Post Corona) 85
  - Observation 2 – No need for perfection anymore, glitches don't matter 87
  - Observation 3 – Isolation versus Intimacy 88
  - Observation 4 – Keep some secrets 90
  - Observation 5 – Strangers through your screen 92
  - Observation 6 – Remote work is the future nobility 93
  - Observation 7 – Mobility is nobility 95
  - Observation 8 – Being an actor versus a reactor 97
  - Observation 9 – From Haves & Have Nots to now Knows & Know Nots 99
  - Observation 10 – Big picturism will be needed 101
  - Observation 11 – Algorithms are making all the decisions (Part 2) 103
  - Observation 12 – Going viral is a short-term goal post 105
  - Observation 13 – Media is lumped together now. Culture is what is separate now. .. 107
  - Observation 14 – How do you see the world? 109
  - Observation 15 – From dead ends to What ifs! 110
  - Observation 16 – Data and The Death Of Random 112
  - Observation 17 – The wild west of falsehood is our new media world 114
  - Observation 18 – Digital content pollution 118
  - Observation 19 – Redefinition of the live event 120
  - Observation 20 – The rise of the immersive media economy 123
  - Observation 21 – We are all bakers now 126
  - Observation 22 – The 2020's and how it will be a whole other world. 129
  - Observation 23 – Normal does not exist anymore 134
  - Observation 24 – Cultural posturing and cultural resonance = Bonus material 136
  - Observation 25 – AI and intellectual property 139
  - Observation 26 – The Gift Wrap 141
  - Observation 27 – The only way is forward 143
  - Observation 28 – My Truth 145
  - Thank you 149
  - Acknowledgements 151

PART 1

To succeed in the 2020's you will have to create meaningful social tension in your work.

I wrote in a conversational tone with a lot of spontaneous thought.
More of a transcription than an edit.

Empower and power are often two words that are discussed in this social and streaming media era we live in currently. I feel they are fraternal twins not identical twins. Let's start with their definitions:

Empower – Authority or power given to someone to do something.

Power – The capability or ability to direct or influence the behaviour of others or the course of events.

I wish to start by saying this is the era of empowerment. You see the word everywhere in the press and media. Everyone is told to take empowerment in this era. Social media and the smart phone in pockets allow someone to publish something for the world to consume. That empowerment comes with fine print though. Unless you have someone or a group listening or reading what you are saying it is all a grand illusion. Just because you are permitted to do something doesn't mean anything happens. The key to all this empowerment is to have a small fertile following or know someone who has a following that will endorse what you are saying.

In this age I feel most people wish to believe that something is good and will spread on its own.

I however know that is a false truth, due to the need to continue this façade of organic traffic, that people continue to believe the possibility of hitting the "viral lottery". Your following/fanbase/subscribers or that endorsement from a relevant voice is the key for idea empowerment in theory.

The whole point of what we are discussing here is people have to care about you or what you are saying by engagement to share it with others, which is the true end in this era.

A share is considered an endorsement. That is the basis of beginning to have power in this age we are in. This is the journey that is going on globally 24/7. The who or what will be guiding others. Where will people get their information from? Where will they derive there entertainment from? Where will they get their education from? In the pages ahead I will be discussing these 2 words and how we are all impacted by them. When people arrive at the destination of when they say "my brand", they will be ready for 2020. The saying my brand is really saying my power.

SEGMENT ZERO

The Ultimate Reality

In this era that we find ourselves in the end game is to keep people dialed into your platform/site/content and or brand. THAT IS IT IN A NUTSHELL. For Google, Facebook, Tik Tok, Snapchat etc. That is the only thing that matters. They must keep you scrolling, searching, interacting, sharing, liking for as long possible. We are the real product make no mistake.

Our goal as individuals is the same as the big boys. We must keep people dialed into our content/sites for as long as possible, so we can win just like they do because if people leave they will probably not come back. With that being said we must ask ourselves what will keep people on your page and platform. That is a very hard question to answer. Due to that reality people are taking various shortcuts that are everywhere. For example, the use of buying views and followers pretends to show that you are popular. These shortcuts cost money yet in the long run does nothing because they are not real people. I always say what are behind the numbers? This also gives the appearance that you have more traffic then you really have. The more traffic you hypothetically show means more monetization for the brand/artist/corporation.

The daily fight is on the newsfeed as everyone wants you to click on what they are offering.

In my business of music people are always trying to out hyperbole the next person. Everyone is living the "reality show" in their daily life now to keep people interested in brand/content or products they may sell due to their brand. An expert on this is the media mogul 50 Cent aka Curtis Jackson. He is what folks call a champion troll master! I noticed with my own eyes when Power the tv series was coming out summer 2019 his trolling expanded rampantly. It keeps him top of mind and people talking and thinking about him. The crucial thing about 50 Cent is that he has something to consume or sell to folks. A lot of people are now just stuck trying to go viral for the sake of trying to go viral. From my experience now before you go viral you need to have a foundation already built so if you go viral you have something to give/show people besides just going viral. Going viral will be forgotten very quickly and replaced by something else in the era we live in. I have realized then that I am in the time business. The longer you spend on my platform/content/brand then I will be able to monetize my media. The tech companies' algorithm will take notice which is ultimately what our goal is! My job is to take as much time from the consumer. From now on I want you to think of yourself as Mark Zuckerberg. Therefore, Facebook ads cost more if you have a link that takes the person away from Facebook. You better get this principle and put it in all of what you are doing going forward. What will be your bread and butter platform? What is its strength versus weaknesses? Remember attention is the commodity you need.

The streaming services are focused on you listening and staying on their platform for as long as possible. The key is not a sales strategy but a consumption strategy. In this world of the algorithm continuous recommendations will be fed to get more consumption. Think of DSP'S like a casino where the house must win because if there is no house it is no casino, right?

Whenever they tweak something it has to be a benefit for them. This makes total sense as you will do the same for your platform. Please understand I am just making clear observations about this.

The tech giants really pretend they are about curation. Curators lead to promotion and marketing to get attention. Curators and creations really don't matter. The algorithm makes the decision. They really don't care about brands. The algorithm doesn't care about you unless it is getting fed by your offerings. To close out this segment and leave you with more to deliberate, I will use this unknown quote. It is hard to be picked by authorities but also for strangers to discover you.

SEGMENT ONE

Only Caterer in Town

One day I realized that this digital era is now catering to what people want or need. In the mass market era we didn't do that. Here is what I mean, I will refer to an old animated TV show called The Flintstones. Fred Flintstone and his best friend Barney are chosen to throw the Water Buffalo party and Fred's daughter Pebble's is having a party. He drives to Cobble Stone caterers and the proprietor is giving smart remarks to Fred who is the customer. Fred gets upset and within the conversation the proprietor says " I am the only caterer in town". On social media there are a zillion caterers who are out there with their content/products/services attempting to get them noticed by all sorts of methods. No one is looking for what you do. You are not the only caterer in town. When you are a monopoly, you can be smug because you are the only caterer in town. I am in the song business and literally over a month there are over a million new ones. Those in music have so many new songs to compete against and let's not bring up the catalogue material, the public is flooded with music. Now people can be choosey. In this time period you must do something to stand out! It all comes and goes. My message is you are not the only caterer in town. Most people online think that they are. People are now overloaded with their own life.

Most do not need something new to fill their time up with unnecessary things. I like to say you "have to be a priority." That is old music label talk. This use to mean that the label would put a "major push" behind you and your song. In this overloaded digital world being a priority now is where a few are. Taylor Swift is one of the lucky few. The goal now is through your set up is to get as many people, entities riding with you when you are launching your content/product/service.

You must show people that they are a priority, so they make you a priority and give you their time from the start. You must assume that everyone else is in this era is the overused B word in this time which is BUSY. You must "unbusy" them.

Final words: The person or people is most important! If you are not catering to them, you will lose them to something or someone else. Be very careful in this social media jungle. Cater to people's desires to relax, be entertained or engage to get your message heard and spread your message.

In my case music is competing on the streaming platform with other art forms. Here is a final thought from a Netflix executive who said that Disney and HBO isn't there biggest rival. SLEEP IS THERE BIGGEST COMPETITION. The only thing we can't make more of is time!!

SEGMENT 2

You do not have to wait

In this digital global media biz, you do not have to wait any more to publish or distribute what you are doing. It is a true game changer for those who use it as such. There are no roadblocks in theory now. The only roadblock is the person or team of people in how they operate. Do they understand the abundance of opportunities that are available daily online? Are you and your team in a heightened opportunity mindset? I am calling it the "human condition" that is holding people up. It is still a process also that will then halt people from financial success. If the team is creatively fertile, they have rampantly increased chances because they are in the "chase". Not having a budget can't stop you from creating. The budget is needed for marketing so you can get your message out to consumers due to the abundance of material. Their financial commitment is necessary. Unless you have the best growth hackers on your team who believe in what you are doing or young enough to have a "digital army" of people who can do coordinated attacks on the web you will have to pay. Younger people usually have the time to know about the latest innovations and hacks that are happening online. As I said prior, you are in the time business so please be very careful what you do with it. The social media companies and the DSP'S know that ultimately, they are in the time business. The systems of these companies are designed to keep you from leaving and more importantly come back frequently.

I am going to discuss simple economics here. We are truly living in a on demand economy especially in the media/content racket. Everything is immediate! Also, the oversupply of content is a crucial element. Your product/service or brand is one of the hundreds of millions now with more being formed as we move into 2020, the true basis of this is how to manage the explosion of data and content which are where the opportunities lie for a brand or entity. You must have the ability to manage all of the things coming at you. By doing that you will be open to opportunities every day. You have the capacity to win. You have the capacity to change your very existence. You have the chance in a symbolic way to hit your own lottery! You must be open to the unknown. To most, the unknown (future) is a scary proposition, but in this online world the unknown and what is next is truly what we are seeking. Roll the dice and go for it with your creativity.

SEGMENT 3

The Age of the unprofessional

Since 2007 there is no debate that the most crucial historic shift has taken place as consumer amateur content that is travelling via social platforms instead of quote unquote "professional media" is the majority of what people ingest now! This has brought about a massive attention and time shift that we are seeing blossom into an ever-changing movement of creators. Facebook, Instagram, YouTube, Tik Tok and Dub smash have become destination and distribution portals for consumption the same way HBO, Showtime, CBS, NBC, ABC were thought about in the immediate past. The professional media of the past which was a closed system now evolved to an open system that now allows anyone to get their message out. The rank and file amateurs that the data centric social media companies need to survive are the crux of this new system. The key to this new system is once something becomes information, it will be and can be shared globally, remixed, reimagined and shared. I say we now live in the continuous remix culture of 21st century creativity as the reinterpretation of the existing works. Digital essentially means modification which has allowed this abundance of viral material. The ability to participate in the changing narrative is so much lower. It is overwhelmingly easier to modify something than to create something from scratch and build it out. To truly understand this and tie in the smart phone in a global backdrop you can begin to see what has happened to the world. You have billions of individuals available to modify. The internet is one giant modifier collectively because once something is turned into digital information it can be adjusted. This has created an unlimited opportunity that literally do not have any financial cost. It only cost the time the person will put in. This is about the enormous amount of creative capital that is available. The phone is the gateway for all of this creativity. For me this has created the age of the ordinary person not the professional star. This is why on the web it is about what and who is next. You never know where it is coming from. This is why also kids are ruling in this world because they have the time to sit around and engage with the latest apps that are always coming out. I like to call this the "casino of content". The age of the ordinary is upon us via the masses around the world who are now empowered. The business has shifted to the normal and ordinary. This group does not want to be promoted to due to what has just been noted. You must create engagement beyond the one-sided element of entertaining and educating. The real tidbit here is when you are producing or creating something the key going forward will be the ability for content to engage. It is a two-sided transaction now. This age of ordinary will create an abundance to entertain friends and family. In the 2020's we begin to see the explosion of content coming from Asia and Africa due to abundance of new creators. With 63% of music searches happening on mobile devices you must make sure your website is ready for mobile platforms in creative businesses especially. The Google algorithm apparently favours content that is accessible via mobile devices.

SEGMENT 4

Data and Advertising Racket

As I have gone through a metamorphosis to becoming a digital citizen, I truly see the present from a digital perspective. As I observe and deliberate on the effects of the digital culture on my daily life and how it effects the economics of life it has come down to fewer and fewer issues. I do not get caught up on the smoke and mirrors of the hardware products like the latest iPhone or coding because I see it basic and simple. That is the key not to be overwhelmed by the technology.

As I ask this question regarding my racket of music what businesses are DSP'S and the social media companies in? The DSP'S a person might say music. For the record DSP"S means digital service provider. Regarding social media companies they might say communications. They are in neither one of those businesses. They are in the data collection and advertising business! We are essentially data slaves because we provide all of this data for free. The only objective is to keep you on their platforms so you can keep producing data for their algorithm. In my eyes this is an ongoing diabolical cycle which is ongoing 24/7. This data is repackaged to then allow us to pay for advertising on the platform due to the on purpose shrinking of organic reach after getting us to spend our time chasing followers and subscribers. Then you add the constantly altered algorithm recipe, the slow death of organic reach is here. Unless you are very large like Rihanna you are not getting much organic support. On Facebook, which is the biggest fish in the pond, organic has shrank to 2 percent. For example, if you have 1000 followers you are reaching 20 people who can see your material. Let me ask you what was the point of spending all that time amassing followers? Get use to the word "algorithm" please. This is how the companies control and prioritize things on the platform. We are the ones feeding it please remember. Every keystroke you do is feeding the algorithm. Here is a crazy thought; what if everyone decided to stay off their phones? Would it stop the feeding frenzy, and would the algorithm go hungry?

Therefore, the battle to keep everyone on a platform is so fierce. Before we leave this subject let's see what the definition of algorithm is: It is a step by step procedure to solve logical and mathematical problems. Think of the Coca Cola formula. The social media and DSP'S do not tell you their algorithm but they are always pushing you to reveal everything online. Please take a time out and deliberate on what I just said. Keep some secrets especially business ones. Take care of your algorithm or recipes that you may control. Please think about what your algorithm may be and protect it.

Addendum July 26th, 2019 in Rolling Stone The two biggest players in the music streaming business Spotify and Apple quietly stopped referring to themselves as music services. Yet they still tout themselves and their millions of songs as the core of their business as they were moving heavily into podcasting. As I always say music was the guinea pig for all of this.

SEGMENT 5

Reach Versus Engagement

So much of what I did in the recent past on any campaign your success was judged on how many people you reached. In the old mass market world how many you reached was the key metric for businesses. On this ever-evolving digital business world reach is now a "vanity metric". It sounds good on paper and in conversation. Saying I reached five hundred thousand sounds like a successful campaign but I will throw a monkey wrench in that statement. In this era of 2020 the crucial metric will be engagement. The reason for that is because if people stopped what they are doing to interact with what you are offering this means you left an impression! Remember I SAID YOU ARE ESSENTIALLY IN THE TIME BUSINESS. The more time people spend on your platform means you have a sliver of their mind. They have given you their most precious commodity which is time in my opinion. Most people may say money but in this online world time is the money. We need engagement, just because you reach someone, and they glance at what you are offering doesn't mean you made a connection with them. I pose the question would you rather reach 500k or have 10k engagement in this era? I would seek out the 10k engagement as the more important metric. The fact consumers had an interaction means they will remember potentially when they see you or your content/product in the future. You may have caused a sale or something of yours was consumed by the individuals. Your campaigns prior to launching should have an emphasis on engagement not reach. You must build it into what you are presenting.

In my opinion you must find a way to personalize what you are doing! Everyone should feel you are speaking to them one on one. Please remember you are not the only caterer in town! Please make sure your campaign is an event! An event captures people in the moment. It feels like something that can't be missed. As the old slogan goes "must see tv". What is the story of the event? Why is the event taking place? The bonus to this is that if people interact, they will share with friends and followers!

This means people outside of your sphere of influence will know about you/product/service/media.

The next level engagement is when people remix your content! This means you have them in your corner. The goal I feel is to get them to remix, restructure and share it to their followers because it is about them. Reach is not something the large media/tech companies can guarantee is real. Globally everyday people are growth hacking their systems and a lot of bots are in place that look real until deeper investigation by the companies which can end up in the news.

It is also quid quo pro. The big companies only do something if it becomes a scandal of sorts and it affects their bottom line with advertisers who are viewing the numbers as real. The companies know about these bot sales all over the internet. The point of these bots is to mimic the human. The machine learning is to mimic a human brain essentially. These fake numbers in my eyes can't be stopped because they feed the business model of more traffic and attention.

Understand the internet is the best place to scam you. The individuals now don't trust the big corporation now but will trust a person with a random Gmail who will sell them something. I will say at least the big brand has something to lose. What does the random email person have to lose?

Always remember these words reputation, integrity and risk in all you do. Please think of this before you engage. If it is too good to be true, then just run the other way. If you are going for reach, go work the official platforms themselves. For example, I would suggest working with Google ads or Spotify ads platform and learn the system so you can develop your own growth hacks. Start small and grow. Remember you are in the time business so put your time in to learn.

Addendum – The MTV video awards have had sinking ratings for years now according to the Nielson's rating service. The VMA'S according to The Hollywood Reporter drew 1.93 million viewers down from 2.25 million in 2018. That is a double-digit percentage decline in tv viewership.

Yet the show saw a significant increase in social and online video views up 85 percent from 2018 according to the data from Conviva Social Insights. The MTV VMA'S collected hundreds of millions of social video views, primarily on owned properties. The show trended for 12 hours straight world wide. In the key demo 25-54 it was up 6 percent and down 6 percent in the 18-49 demo. Depending on what you are focusing on you can and will come up with a different assessment. I find the two metrics clashing. If you look at the Nielson's MTV is falling and can't get up. If you go by social numbers MTV is still relevant and doing their business.

SEGMENT 6

Discovery vs. A Hit

In this streaming era of music where the algorithms are more important than the human curator and with musical abundance, the idea of the hit record is changing quickly. With more and more music available people just have no time to even know if new music is out now. Music is now competing with all other media categories which also includes games. Also, with the mass market only available for an exclusive few a hit can be somewhat unattainable. My personal focus is on discovery of the song and then hopefully the artist. The way music is now becoming more dependent to playlist culture it is harder to break an artist. I am saying now with the song and the artist separate from each other you must do separate campaigns. Therefore, even Universal Records with a global footprint and billions in the kitty does not A&R an artist and build from them from scratch. It can't be done on sensible financials and the patience is not there. The technology that we glorify took care of that. It is the elephant in the room that the music industry (big three labels) and the DSP'S who pretend they are about music won't discuss because it is bad for the business perception to the customers. Record labels have a negative connotation and rightfully so but they also crafted The Beatles, Aretha Franklin, Rolling Stones, Whitney Houston, Elvis Presley, Elton John, Stevie Wonder, Jackson 5 and Frank Sinatra. Playlists have become the new album. You can have a playlist and listen and just keep bopping your head. Just one of the many songs available. With that being the case getting the song and artist to a consumer in an organic fashion is crucial due to streaming there are no old songs anymore. Your catalogue of songs is available for a person to learn about you and them. Let's use the hottest artist as I write Lizzo as an example. Her two hottest songs came out in 2017 and 2016. The one song Truth hurt's became number one in the USA 2 years after the fact. This means to me that you are not just in the latest release biz. Due to the fact that DSP'S are not in the music business, discovery is a much more compelling option for people to consider. Any song is open to be liked. People only care that they like it not that it came out last Friday or that it came out 10 years ago. This means old songs can be new again. You just must share it with people. You can remix it under a new backing track so people can discover it as a new piece of material. This also makes your catalogue much more active and more valuable in this streaming era. I recently saw a Kanye West song from 2002 having gone platinum in 2019. This made me realize that even with a big artist brand like Kanye West discovery can take place. Due to streaming/commercials/movies songs are constantly being needed by producers of stories. Abundance of opportunity is upon us with all these new media platforms. What is old is new again.

Now think about this, I say to people music is now in your pocket. The DSP'S have millions of songs that they have available that people can bump across randomly in theory. But the reality is it must come from somewhere. Why would they randomly look for the song and artist? The record label/artist can be caught off guard now. Discovery is dictating things, not the label or artist.

Another example when an artist puts out an album now the old school mentality is to pick the single. Now a lot of big artists such as J Cole just drop the album without prior promo and let the fans find their favourite song. Now the label doesn't try to force the hit record down people's throats and shoot the video to find out that they picked the wrong song to be the single.

Discovery is also a money saver and saves you from a PR disaster. As an independent, I still A&R a single but when I release a full length, I will follow suit with what I said above. Let the people pick the priority song!

SEGMENT 7

The Push and Pull

This was a song by the singer Rufus Thomas which was a dance craze for a moment decades ago. In this digital era with streaming taking over it is now less push and much more pull! Let me explain…In the mass media era marketeers and business use to push people into things. There was a limited amount marketing/distribution channels and it took a large amount of capital to implement. I will speak from the music biz perspective here. Radio used to be the way songs were found by people and print magazines/newspapers. I am speaking before the year 1981 and the birth of MTV. Pushing things at people was the plan! The tool was rotation where you would here the song every 3-4 hours which by the end of that first week people would be singing the song or humming it without them knowing they were doing it. In this digital streaming era of on demand we are not pushing anymore because pushing will not work with this generation. They watch things/listen to things when they want to. An example is binge watching which was made a thing by Netflix. That is a pull not a push. You must pull people in now not push people to you and your content/media. The customer is in control now! It all boils down to if they like what you are presenting to the marketplace. I want to add the cost of your media/content doesn't matter! It is all about how it connects with the consumer. We are in the "Hunger Games" of content/media if you really want to look at. At this stage of the game as we move into 2020, we are not chasing the TV and radio gatekeepers at all. That comes much later if it comes at all. In this era, you don't need them. You need those followers/subscribers who will hopefully become fans to catapult you to the next level to being a credible and relevant brand. The key is to keep them enthused and to mobilize them to share what you offer. The big end is for them to create content based on your content.

Going forward you will have to look at the mobile phone as going into someone's home or personal space. You are going one-on-one with that person. You must visualize this so you understand the gravity of the situation. At its most powerful the connection (emotionally) whether shared virtually on a streaming platform or live at concert is the end game. The internet is not a mass market tool. It looks like it is because in theory you can reach billions, but it is a micro medium. It also a direct marketing channel. Before we end this segment, here is the key I feel: When people say my followers…

my subscribers...they forget you do not own them. It is a PRIVILEGE THEY GIVE YOU TO SEND THEM SOMETHING. THEY CAN UNFOLLOW OR UNSUBSCRIBE.

They like something about you or your content/message you put out. PLEASE REMEMBER IT IS A PRIVILEGE NOT OWNERSHIP.

SEGMENT 8

15 Second racket

We now live in something I call the "I never heard of you syndrome" yet the person or brand has millions of followers/subscribers. It was said that everyone is seeking their "15 minutes of fame" in the old mass media world. Due to the advent of Tik Tok I now must alter this to 15 seconds of fame! It is maddening now that with the device in your pocket and the capability to download a few apps you can now get your 15 seconds whenever and however! A permanent "Hunger Games" of fame gathering. This generation of kids are going for there 15 seconds and some are turning it into a business before they graduate high school. This streaming/social media world has now created the age of the influencer. I come from the music biz who in my mind are the original influencers. That was the whole point. Someone liked a song of a person and then it happened...they were Influenced. That music personality had a fan base. Now it is followers or subscribers in this era. It all had to be very organized with capital and the mass media tools for that person to become what was called a tastemaker. They made taste and more importantly changed tastes. The taste changer in my eyes is the big power. This is where the music artist still maintains a lead. That song is the ultimate influencer and power to that lies with the music artist. An amazing thing that is happening now is you can have the "I never heard of you syndrome" because the person or brand maybe only large on that platform but outside of that platform they are unknown. NICHE FAME is the new thing in this app culture that has taken over from the mass media outlet. You have this permanent 15 second culture which is happening everywhere every day. If you go to these apps you can just go and see who or what is trending. THAT IS THE GOAL NOW TO TREND IN THESE 15 SECOND FAMES WORLD. It doesn't really have to have substance! Your goal is just trend.

    This has created the meme/emoji/gif culture you can debate and argue. In 2018 –2019 meme culture took over. A correctly curated meme can take over a narrative. We are at the point of major meetings are being held about memes in agencies. I will admit I felt that this was stupid and miss the wave. I didn't take it seriously, but I have changed...lol. The amazing interns that I worked with in the last 2 years changed my whole perspective. I am now a meme adherent. They are discussed at marketing meetings. This is now a culture which is crucial in the "ATTENTION ECONOMY" we live in currently. The continuous miniaturization of content and media is altering how you get your message out to the world. You must understand this in 2020 and beyond. I am speaking about the music biz but it can be applied to any media or content...I know I have 7 seconds to get someone to continue with what I am presenting to them. I want to say this to close this segment; what business am I in? In 2020 I am in the time business primarily. Think about that regarding your business or lifestyle.

SEGMENT 9

Famedom versus Stardom

This 15 second lifestyle has created the microwaveable viral moment I am labelling FAMEDOM. I do not call it stardom because in my eyes to become a star is a diligent process that takes years with a lot of luck and immense belief to get you through those dark days you will face. It cannot be microwaved despite what is being placed in the media to entice people to chase it. This 15 second viral moment has created a dangerous precedent because people now mix up famedom with stardom. The problem to me with famedom is that people try to extend it to stardom and do not realize stardom is very detailed and takes a dedicated team. It is not something that comes from the microwave! It comes from the slow cook oven! To fully understand please compare a microwaveable soup to a thanksgiving turkey. Please stop and meditate on this for a moment. I will say that the tech/social media/DSP'S have the masses of the globe chasing famedom you can get via social media/tech content companies. If you want stardom you will need professional management and the old-line companies in the music industry or Hollywood who have that DNA knowledge. You must understand the differences between Brad Pitt, George Clooney, Beyonce, Rihanna, Katy Perry and Taylor Swift. Those individuals were groomed for stardom not famedom. I implore you to get books on 1940's -1960's Hollywood to understand and the music industry from 1960's -1990's to understand the level of investment dollars and time that went into making a star. These companies do have a bad rep for their contracts, especially the music ones and I agree with that aspect of the narratives. On the flipside, they did create some magic that lives on. That is the point of what we do I feel which to make memorable moments that go on. Do not just live in the microwave. Make sure you slow cook yourself.

SEGMENT 10

Social Capital

The chase for "social authority" in 2020's will be more intense than in the decade of 2010's due to your "digital voice" will be your business life source. Now what will come with this pursuit of "social authority"? I feel the chase for likes, comments, followers, views that gives the individual more of it will continue but get worse as digital becomes more of how we do business. A study of how prevalent this has infested social media was done by investigating a cross-section of the biggest music artist brands on the planet. You would think the numbers they possess would be real but hold on! I was shocked by what I read. The study was based on their Instagram and Twitter accounts. Here is a brief example of what was found to give us a brief perspective:

BTS had 47% of fake followers, Taylor Swift had 46% of fake followers, Ariana Grande had 46% of fake followers, Miley Cyrus had 45% of fake followers, Katy Perry had 44% of fake followers, DJ Marshmello had 43% of fake followers, Jennifer Lopez had 45% of fake followers, Nicki Minaj 39% of fake followers, Drake had 36% of fake followers, Ed Sheeran had 35% of fake followers. This is a brief sample, but it gives you reading here a perspective. I hope you decide now to develop your base the old fashion way. Do the work! Do the one-on-one interactions. Keep releasing media that drives people to connect with you and share your work with others. The numbers should have a real person behind them not a Bot which gives the appearance of a real person. Please go research what a Bot is if you do not know. People are talking more about fake news than fake data or numbers. In my world that fake data is just as critical. This fake data is allowing people to call themselves influencers, brand ambassadors etc to monetize this fake social capital and with everyone shifting over to the digital world as we go into the 2020's all I can say is look out. In my eyes due to the human condition for shortcuts so pervasive, more and more of this behaviour is expected. Let me say this to you would you want 1,000 real connections or the appearance of 50k followers? The large celebrities mentioned will be fine because they really have the ability to sell out arenas, stadiums and set streaming records that validate their social capital. I would say most of us here can't do that. You need to show that you have some social authority via engagement, well done media/content and release it on a consistent basis so people will see you and hopefully take notice. I would say it will take a diligent 3-5 years for most but for those who can engineer or create a viral moment would accomplish social authority much quicker. I want to thank Bobby Owsinski of music 3.0 for bringing this out to the public. To really put the tombstone on purchasing these fake social authority sponsors. large brands and media companies now possess software to see if your social authority is real. During the 2010-2012 period of the wild west I know record labels got burned by some of this fake authority. You don't want to get caught cheating now because it very bad for business. It is not the volume of people you influence but who you influence that truly matters.

SEGMENT 11

The death of Editorial

We live in the paywall now. As we speed into 2020, I have had to accept the death of editorial. With music being viewed as a commodity and the oversupply of it bloggers, DJ'S journalists don't really want your music unless it comes with a compelling story. Your new song/album/video is not news anymore. That will apply to anything that has been digitized. During the last 3 years I took it on the chin thinking my pitch mattered. I still was coming from an editorial perspective when now it is marketing or sponsored content. I was saying judge it on it's worth. However, for people to judge it they would have to look at it. If no one looks at it then it can't be a story. With the oversupply of content/media this has made people put up a paywall. I understand it now! You must pay people for their time now with the shift to a gig/app economy due to the technology. Now you must pay people to do what used to be judged on the merits of the media or content. That for the most part is over with. Everyone isn't paying however. The big brands don't pay due to the fact they will bring traffic to the person's platform.

Many bloggers that I used to send media and pitches to for years now won't look at it unless you go through their paywall. I totally understand it though. This cuts down on many pitches they will get and allow them to focus on the ones that matter. This fact totally alters the process of getting your new material out and your budget for marketing. A close friend of mine calls it the PayPal economy! This behaviour means we are all in the marketing world. The sad part about this is that you must be careful on how you spend your capital. There are frauds and charlatans in the online marketing world. Everyone doesn't have integrity. This means that everything you see online I am saying is sponsored. Nothing is just going on because it is good. Sponsorship is behind it.

This brings me to your fan base who will support you when you give them something. Your diehard fans/followers will become your editorial team now. They support without the paywall because they are anticipating your media release. Hopefully your fans/followers will share it to allow it to spread around organically. You can ask them to do specific things for you. If you have taken care of them they will listen to you probably. Attach something to your media release to get them excited!

Get it to them first! Ask them for their input which will give them the impression that they are part of your release. That is crucial to get that fan editorial.

SEGMENT 12

Traditional advertising 2020

With traditional unsolicited advertising the objective was to spread the message everywhere and to interrupt people. That is something that I feel a tombstone is needed. If you accept the concepts, the thoughts and information I have put forth then you will stop paying for general advertising.

Also, your spending on ads needs to be redirected to other mechanisms. Technology is ruling now.

People can use ad blockers which means they will not see your ad. I am still a person who doesn't block things because I am still seeking that random intangible piece of information. I know most people are not like that now. The age of the email blast is also kind of antiquated with email blocker technology and in Europe with the GDPR legislation. You can't pitch like before. A lot of it goes to the spam section and not being seen. I spoke to an email marketer recently and I was shocked that he had rates like it was 2005. I was amazed but he was doing a brisk business apparently. This told me people were still doing this enough that he was prospering.

I used to do cold calling for a stockbroker when I thought I wanted to be a stockbroker in my younger years. The cold call was the weapon of choice. As we move into 2020 with the cell phone being so common with caller ID, people just don't pick up anymore and if they do are usually not to friendly. In the age of I am so busy and overwhelmed with information from my social newsfeed people don't want to talk to you. Increasing the spend probably won't help you! I look at it as throwing money into an abyss. However, the increase in spend gives us a false sense of security.

In 2020 I feel it is absolutely no time for that.

SEGMENT 13

Future is fragmented and miniature during 2020's

The definition of things will be forever evolving in a much quicker fashion in the culture of brand development as we move forward. The way social media and streaming platforms deliver content/media to people via recommendations based on their preferences is truly putting the final epitaph on the mass market star. IT IS TIME TO DEVELOP THE NICHE STAR. I feel that if you go hard into your niche utilizing the social and streaming companies you can make a real good living as the middle class global aggregated brand becomes more prevalent. The key will be to aggregate your followers/subscribers/fans with all the tech available to you. For example, if you have 35k in North America, 30k in Europe,15k in Asia, 5k in Australia and 20k in Africa that is a total of 105k potential touch points. Compared to Rihanna that is miniscule, but those people have shown an interest in you and decided to stay in touch with you. If you reach 15-20 percent of your followers consistently that is like doing an arena in any major market. In my case it would be Madison Square Garden. Imagine if you can monetize on those 15-20 thousand people at 35 dollars a pop.

How much is that? That is a pretty decent living if you can do that twice a year. The 2020's will be about these smaller/miniature business model for the artist/creator brand. You will be reaching them directly and through the newsfeed. Your goals will change. Instead of reaching everyone you will need to reach the right ones because there will be no advances of money. You will have to sell and monetize all of what you are doing. You will be a global entrepreneur! The audience however has shown a proclivity for you and what you present which will increase your odds for success because it will not be a cold situation. This the strategic shift that the music artist will have to do and for that matter any artist/entrepreneur. With the tech/streaming companies being the "invisible hand" along with the algorithm you will now play your hand on what those companies are saying is hot. In this world there is much less room for randomness in your operations. Instead of broadcasting you should be narrowcasting to your base of people.

With the massive increase of creators and the permanent battle for time and attention what is already known will have a distinct advantage. If something or someone has been a success in the past and is still relevant I feel they will become a safe haven for the consumer. We are already seeing this in Hollywood with all the sequels and extensions of movies. Your personal brand will become an oasis in a desert of creation. Collaborations with your followers/subscribers/fans to utilize that powerful and latent force I feel will become much more popular with forward thinking brands. If you go back to the discussion of the remix, then you know you must be vigilant to be aware what is happening on your platforms. Nostalgia is a very powerful marketing tool along with thinking globally. However, moving locally will be very essential in the 2020's. Reputation will be essential to the survival of what you are doing especially in this fake news and inauthentic period. Let's face it, anybody can put up anything and appear to be whatever now. I want to say social media breeds inauthentic activities because there are no gatekeepers now. Do not waste these important factors in any trivial way. The artist must have a voice that sends a clear message of ownership of the message/media or content as we go to 2020. The keys will be a digital brand, your relationship with your fans and using the data to make the best decisions because you are always moving forward. This will be an amazing time to be a creative artist brand with proper brand management.

This will be a time to B2C (Business to consumer) because it will be so personal in my eyes. Personal connection whether text/email or direct messaging will be part of the fan experience. Live streaming your branded events will be more boffo! People will be tuning into your personal branded experiences. THE SMALLER AND INTIMATE THE BETTER. Whoever is there will look to be special and connected. People will be tuning in via there phone. In 2020 everything is going in reverse…create events that amplify the digital. Orchestrate that physical and digital event as one.

People will be immersed in you and all things you. One place to reach and send your global audience to. Think of the money that is spent on travel, hotel, per diems and other expenses that can be put into a stationary set design. Meditate on that prior to your next tour.

VR apps are being used by people to watch music festivals. An example of this is the festival The Wireless doubled the amount of people watching and consuming the event. According to the report 130k went in person but 250k watched on the Melody VR app which works on smart phones and VR headsets like the Oculus and Samsung. The app gives people an audience experience without having to stand in the audience according to the Forbes article dated July 22nd, 2019. For me this means you as a branded performer had better start thinking about the phone (as I call them now a P.E.D Personal Entertainment Device) and that can be a lucrative business with your global audience.

Touring will always be the best way to touch people but until then you can still connect with those people to get them dialed in with you.

SEGMENT 14

Future comes fast

In this era of innovation and constant disruption the future comes fast. The future is speeding up and this will make things tougher due to the abundance of things happening at once now. My question is how do you prioritize where you put your time and thoughts?

For me, Amazon is having a compelling effect on how things are done going forward. Just think about Amazon Prime and how it has transformed behaviour and consumer choice. But the big thing is good old Alexa spearheading voice technology. The tentacles of Amazon reach far and wide.

Alexa is leading the pack on voice and due to this I am formulating plans on how to tie-n Alexa in my marketing schemes. Prime now has 100 plus million members. Amazon's footprint in media and music is growing yearly. Their influence in these areas is to monitored closely. Alexa will definitely alter how I do marketing. I have already developed a few things which I will incorporate in 2020. What is scary in theory to me is voice will assist the big powerful brands because they are top of mind to 100's of millions of people. The coming battles for micro brands will be how do you become top of mind in this voice activated world? I feel nichification will be a primary tool for micro brands. You will have to have top of mind in a few people's mind. That starts with your followers/subscribers/fans. That is the micro brand first line of offense. You must go inside out not outside in. The consumer can say Alexa find me that brand. TRUE OWNERSHIP OF A SPACE WILL BE NECESSARY FOR BUSINESS SURVIVAL. 2020 WILL BE THE AGE OF STANDING OUT AND STANDING FOR SOMETHING SO YOU DO NOT BLEND IN. IF YOU BLEND IN YOU WILL BE LOST IN THE CONFUSION. Smart speakers in the USA are growing exponentially. However, if you extrapolate the trend globally in the 2020's when discussing your brand/artist/product/service you must be part of the trend to stay relevant. I will say that I agree with some futurists that there will be less keyboards and typing on phones. As I am planning my first mainland China release of music I will have to get the translation for our artist brand and songs. According to studies the average person can type 40 words per minute. The average human can speak 150 words per minute. Based on those numbers where do you think this is headed? With the world caught up in efficiencies and I know that we are in the time business, this is just the tip of iceberg starting in 2020. It will behoove all of us to dig into our mind and open it up to any possibilities. I would like to thank Mangrove Capital partners for amazing awe-inspiring research. Even after saying all of that I will now say Alexa is not your focus.

The technology is not your focus even though the technologist will have you thinking it is what is most Important. You must keep up with what is happening in technology so you can troubleshoot it to see how your brand can use it or not use it. However, I feel it is more important to develop the most compelling content that the human customer says Alexa please find me blah blah blah. In my Case Find TRAEDONYA'S song Hollywood or Find A.K Smith-Ford's book Live Digital or Be Irrelevant.

Personal branding is your top priority. Making the most compelling media/content and messages will be what you must do to get that top of mind of the consumer.

This way the consumer goes wow who is behind that! I feel due to the concentration of power by the Facebook's, Amazon, Google's on the western side of the world people will be seeking that closer human personal connection through that device in our pocket. I will close by saying the technology will come and go. To make sure you can really see this I will bring up Beethoven and Mozart. Their music is still around. The technology from their time is in the Smithsonian. Don't get to enamoured with technology. Use it to your advantage as a tool but it comes and goes. Just giving you a perspective so you will know where to put your time and energy as we navigate this very pulsating time in the 2020's. People who are willing to LIVE DIGITAL and adapt with the constant disruption as a way of life now will be prosperous during these times.

SEGMENT 15

Equity of Experiences

In life we build up equity in all types of things just from being on this earth. I am attempting to dial specifically, into my sum total of life experiences that are in my conscious and more importantly my subconscious. That is your personal algorithm that can feed you recommendations to make better decisions. Those things are something that you own. The question for every single person with an entrepreneurial nature is to dive into that "EQUITY OF EXPERIENCES" we all have that are unique to each person. That equity most of us do not harvest! It is something only the person can reference! It is an intangible that can't be touched by others because only you have walked through your life. What I am discussing here is not something we think about. but for myself on the way to "digital citizenship" I am dialling into. We all have our catalogue of equity. As we move into the 2020 era your own intangible equity will become much more valuable. That is a free asset category that people don't delve into. You have to take the time to harvest it. This can be anything that you can reference and utilize as a growth hack, as you move in this new era of billions of creators. Take the time to build your own reference library. It can be a reference from kindergarten. It can be a reference from a conversation with your grandfather.

A conversation with a teacher. I am trying to get you to open things up inside of yourself.

I will discuss two very prevalent points that you can reference to show what I am attempting to accomplish here. Let's discuss shortcuts, which due to the human condition, we just love them even though they end up costing us more in the long run. We own many instances, but do we refer to them when a shortcut comes along in your life? However, this is when we can dive into the equity we possess or do we dive into another shortcut that takes you further away from what you are trying to accomplish. With all those past references to say been there and done that or do you keep chasing false hopes due to the element of desperation which most people perceive in there moments of challenging situations? Shortcuts takes us to the back of the line. Let's discuss the "diet pill syndrome" how every year there is some new shortcut in the market to help people lose weight in an unhealthy fashion to acquire what you wish in a short-term mindset. Despite all the facts about the human body available, millions of people still believe they can lose real weight fast. That smart phone in your pocket has all of the information needed on that subject to lose weight correctly. You must think about it, if it took people many years to gain the weight, why would they still believe they can lose it in a short period? If you can't take the time to do what you say you want to do, I feel you will keep seeking shortcuts that will keep sending you to the back of the line. The human condition of greed, fear, envy, lust, pride and ego will always take from you the ultimate resource of time. Please use your equity that you already have paid for. You own your "personal reference library".

SEGMENT 16

Why songs will be important in 2020's

In this era, the song from the professional recording artist will be even more important than in the past to get a message through the clutter of messages/media/content that will be published every moment every day from all over the world. A song is a short story that can resonate with someone and hold the attention of people many times over. If a person connects with a song and hopefully the artist through a smart phone there can be a bond formed which can go on for a lifetime.

Madonna's song Vogue is played every day somewhere on the planet. A song brings a moment to you based on a truthful connection. It provides a memory that can provide a visual thought in your mind. Pick a song that you connect with, where does it take you to?

A song can bring attention to your brand and service. Why do Apple and Nike find that song for their commercials? Why do they partner with that song? Even those juggernauts need to bring attention to what they are doing. Even with billions of dollars these companies possess it is no guarantee of attention.

A song is also the ultimate level of free speech. Artistic freedom is a treasured element in society.

The artist is the conscience of society. That freedom has bought attention to many social listeners over the decades that no one else could. The artist doesn't have societal limitations placed on them usually. However, in this new corporate tech/media environment that privilege is being encroached upon. The best thing to bring people together is a concert! Look at how many people will come together for a music festival in person and now through streaming the event in real time.

It brings people of all walks of life together for that common moment. Let's look at how Woodstock in 1969 is now acknowledged as a seminal moment in history not just a concert. Music or a song speaks to society and for society! It can be used as a mirror that can be referred to as part of a historical construct. I feel with billions of creators coming onto the web a song will become more powerful as a means to get a message and moment out to people so they can remember it. Talent in this age will be at a premium and make a huge comeback.

SEGMENT 17

The wrap up

The fight for those that end up on this page of this narrative will be the fight for relevance not popularity in the 2020's. Let's look at the definitions:

Relevance – The quality or state of being closely connected or appropriate.

Popular – Intended for or suited to the taste, understanding, or means of the general public rather than specialist or intellectuals.

If you look at the definitions and you look at the content and context of this narrative, I am discussing relevancy for you. From here you can now tailor your marketing and PR towards the game of relevancy. Leave popularity to the billion-dollar businesses.

YOU WILL NEED AN INNER TEAM! WITHOUT THIS, CREATIVITY AND TALENT CAN BE DELAYED OR OBSTRUCTED IN THE 2020'S. This team needs to be small. Here is a note when Instagram sold to Facebook, they had 13 full time employees.

I see a "gynormous" flood of content on the horizon! If we think it was a lot during this past decade then brace yourself for what is coming due to one compelling trend: The rural areas in Asia, Africa and Latin America will be outfitted with smart phones. This will increase local /regional media and content. Once the low-cost data plans and the multitiered pricing plans get to these areas mass consumption will take place. The crucial trend that must come will be mass creation! Talking billions of people. AI (cheaper software) will give them the new creative tools to do this. For example, currently only 10% of Indian population is consuming music. The number of digital music users is set to go up to 400 million by 2022 creating an unprecedented marketing opportunity. There will be more people calling themselves an artist or more likely a creator. Here is a formula:

Creations + distribution = potential monetization The tools are there for the next global superstar to come from this area of the world. I will be following the trail of this. I suggest people shift their opinions, racist attitudes that will limit their opportunities. Culture will be the only way to succeed.

What I have put together in this narrative is my own continuous "RASHAMON EFFECT". I have put together a framework of thinking, knowing, and remembering that will be needed to survive and prosper in this coming 2020 epoch of abundance of media and content. This will be my reference bible for this epoch that is coming upon us and I hope it is yours in this permanency of attention disruption. I am totally embracing the future (mystery). It will always deliver something and surprise you with opportunities. TREAT THE FUTURE AS A CLEAN SLATE. IF WE LIVE DIGITAL PROBLEMS ARE DISPOSABLE. SOLVING PROBLEMS IN THIS EPOCH CAN BE COUNTERPRODUCTIVE. Dispose and move towards the future.

To close, relevant brands not popular brands will definitely do the most compelling marketing messages in the 2020's. Influencing will be when the consumer/user tell their followers that they like something or dislike something. In the past companies routinely told people why they should like their products/services/ content or media. YOU WILL NEED YOUR FANS/FOLLOWERS/SUBSCRIBERS OR GROUPS. THIS HAS BEEN FUN AND THANK YOU FOR READING AND SUPPORTING ME.

SEPTEMBER 21$^{ST\ 2019}$ 4:11pm

PART 2

THE 2020'S:
BILLIONS WILL CREATE/CONSUME/CONNECT FROM THEIR POCKET

DIGITAL RELEVANCE CAN'T BE BOUGHT BUT IT CAN BE MANIPULATED

The end is your new beginning. I have used myself as an experimental subject in regards to changing myself "mid-flight" while embarking on this personal and business innovation procedure. It took me the time similar to a four year college degree. The process has brought about a series of weekly aha moments" over the years. I like to view it as I had no navigator during my flight.

I am finally delivering this manuscript on 8/20/20. I will call this my graduation day into the "jeopardy economy". The reason why I have decided to give the economy that name is because once you consume the information in the narrative you will see maybe you are in jeopardy. The concepts/trends and the "sleight of hand" I am discussing here are activities the masses of individuals have no idea is happening to them. I knew something was different in 2015 but I couldn't put my finger on it. What I postulate here has taken me a little time to accept. The acceptance is the hard part. If you go through this whole narrative, I will save you a lot time. You will see I talk about that four-letter word a lot in the narrative.

As I watch another election come up, I see the same nonsense being done to the American people. There is no mention of what is really happening to them and what will happen to them unless people decide to change how they view the world. In 2016 Hillary Clinton nor Donald Trump mentioned the subjects in this narrative. Maybe they didn't know, but that is what political advisors on staff are for I feel. We are now in 2020 about to embark with Trump versus Biden via a backdrop of an unprecedented corona pandemic and the protest movement due to the murder of George Floyd at the hands of the Minneapolis police. I see nothing coming from either party or candidate.

During these four years I truly see the world from a different perspective. I am definitely not the same person. On a very personal level it is very hard to have the same old tired and redundant discussions that lead me down the same wormhole to zero gains. Due to the subjects I discuss in this narrative the individual does not have the time to waste. Every "structural system" of operation is affected by what I discuss here. Whether you are rich or poor, smart or stupid, you will be affected and can't dodge this situation. That is what gives me the heebie-jeebies. You will not be protected as you were in the past economies. Prejudicial behaviours of all kinds will not protect like they did in the past. Those behaviours of racism, sexism, genderism or religious bias will not help you as much. These have protected certain people since the genesis of this nation.

It is absolutely no more time for people to look to leaders who are not telling what is really coming to disrupt your life. I have decided to be pro-active and have accepted it is up to how I view the world on a daily basis. I didn't explain what I was contemplating to others because I saw that people for the most part wouldn't understand. Panic, fear and all of the other elements of the human condition would kick in. People do mean well but they can only view the world through the prism of their life. Most can't or won't make an attempt to question you after listening. Most of us are judgemental and live in the world of blame, fault or fear instead of asking the questions of depth that matter in the moment. The people closest to you will be the ones I am speaking about.

I went out outside of my sphere of influence. Went out of the safety zone, where most of us stay. Outside of the financial loans that kept me just above sea level, I knew I couldn't be helped or more importantly get the proper assistance needed. I had to go way off the reservation of safety. Once I started, I saw it would be deep dive into challenging every one of my ideals and ideas. Once I started, I knew it would be a grind to somewhere else. As you get older you think you know where that somewhere is. I found out however, you really don't know.

The concept of the unknown has to become a positive comfortable place in order to prosper in the 2020's. I will give you a little background of myself here, I never finished college, based on my own volition. Once I got there, I saw it wasn't for me but more importantly I saw that it would not get me where I wanted to go. I can look back now and I see that I "tossed the playbook" early in my life. I am right now asking people to toss their playbook here in this narrative. I am using myself as a beacon and a tour guide.

If you are reading this, I do not pull any punches. The concepts/ideas will challenge everything about yourself and maybe your life. In CEO suites they are calling what I am saying here "the reset of the economy". I propose here that the individual reset themselves in less time than it took myself to create what I have conceived for myself called Living digital or be Irrelevant. Time is your most precious currency, so please get started asap. You will see repetitive things in here that I decided to leave in so you can see the growth over time and how crucial to our life these subjects are. I wrote this staggered over time. After I had published my first narrative, I saw it was so much to say on this idea of living digital. It also shows the overwhelming amount of information that is crucial that you can forget because so much is coming at you. I found this to be a great way to show my journey and the common threads of my message. Please remember, when you are playing a game you can't win, the best thing is not to try harder but play another game. Change the game people.

I will set the tone for the narrative by two quotes. Here they are:

It has never been made easier for humans to believe the beautiful lie than a difficult truth. -Unknown source

In this narrative I will explore this difficult truth that we do not wish to here.

I watched a Ted Talk by the actor Ethan Hawke on 8/12/20 2:20pm on creativity. The compelling statement he said was this:

There is no path till you walk it.

I was knocked out by the simple sentence. Let's walk this together everyone as we get our mind (brain) to ingest only positive fuel from any situation, which will allow yourself to see things in an ever fluid lens. I grew up on Star Wars and I say here "may the force be with you". 8/15/20 11;42am.

INTRODUCTION

This narrative was written to assist in explaining the flow of the new media ecosystem in regards to releasing media/content with an emphasis on music. I wanted to provide some type of deliberation to people so that they can have a higher success rate. This is not the ultimate guide because no such thing exist. This narrative is based on my day-to-day experiences while prepping to release new music and premiere content segments. It is based on real world experiences! It is designed to hopefully save the readers time and money, and stimulate their own thoughts on this subject. The narrative will show you how you fit in this eco system. It will become a referral system when you fall off track, because we all do. I want you to always question when you speak with someone about your business and brand. The narrative will cut down the clutter in the marketplace and allow you to focus on what is necessary. The goal is to have you ready to just focus on your creative juices and not all of the distractions that are around you. The information here will allow you to go to battle every day and get your media out in the most efficient ways. I want to assist giving people a chance to succeed and not get discouraged. Discouragement can be a powerful force and can stop individuals from seeing the positive in all that they are doing.

You are living in the age of artistic creative innovation. THERE ARE REALLY NO RULES! Yet there are principles. The external roadblocks have been removed. The only gatekeepers are in your own mind and your surroundings. Your message and media can get beyond your immediate surroundings but with that also comes responsibilities. This narrative helps you remove any internal roadblocks that you may have. This is my second narrative that I have written during my evolution that I have gone through and I am now practicing what I preach. When I look at the marketplace I now see a lot of nonessential activities. This was written for the creative/artistic person not for the industry person. Once you know where you fit in, it will help you deal with all that will be coming at you. You will now know to be very diligent in anything you are thinking about doing in your business. Chapters 9,10 and 11 are critical to all music artists. So please spend time there and now let's dive in.

CHAPTER 0

Connection Economy

The music/media/content economy is based on instant data movement, hyperconnectivity and hyper flow of information. The rules that used be etched in stone are now everyday becoming less and less meaningful. All of these rules become distant daily for me. All that we are doing now is to create a two-way dialogue with your niche community. You are seeking feedback! The more feedback you acquire tells you that your media has stickiness.

The fans are communicating and talking through channels that are of no cost to them. You need to monitor all of these systems! This is where you shift your attention and time to. It is not based on the industry big voice but the many voices and interactivity of the direct to fan model.

The bulk of programming and vetting decisions are in the hands of machine logic which is controlled by the fans interacting with your media. THIS IS WHAT YOU NEED! You need to create a two way with the fans. On Spotify it is fans adding you to playlists and on Pandora artist station adds; on social media it is shares, likes, mentions to launch yourself and media. Brands are now networks! You are seeking as many opportunities to create a dialogue in this hyper flow environment. So, the more you create, you increase getting the consumer's attention!

From now on this ecosystem is set up to feed single pieces of media not multiple pieces!

In this new media system, you must be open to keep learning, adapting and reinventing! You are always learning on the fly. You truly never know what will happen. You must embrace this connection economy and not the industrial economy of old.

We live in a constant use of imagination, intuition and innovation. In this connection economy on a daily basis you never know what, where, when, and who is coming. You are always connecting,

and creating media for that future moment! You will now be constantly questioning ideas, belief systems or tenets in your industry of media creation and delivery. No more failure, just learning! With the constant structural innovation we have to keep a very open mindset. I can see now this will be our true challenge to stay relevant not popular! In the digital entertainment world we are after relevance because people will be looking and listening to your media. You must figure out, what may make the audience return to your channels. We are all in the "AUDIENCE SHARE" pursuit. I will state here, we are all chasing ratings for our own media just like HBO, Showtime, CBS, NBC and ABC. Now please meditate on that. With the amount of choice that is out there due to the digital media explosion consumers have an infinite amount of choices to take up their time and attention! So how do you handle that? You must be honest here and think about it! Spotify statistics said that ten percent of their very active users are in discovery mode! Now let's stop for a second and meditate! Now let's continue...this means that consumers are going for what they know! Now back to the 10 percent thing for a moment... that is the segment you need to get to! These are the people who want new, emerging and undiscovered artists. That stat scared me personally and it should scare you! This means at any given moment the majority of people are seeking known quantities not unknown, you can extrapolate that across the board and apply this to many businesses. You must ask, how are you making consumers feel? Just like on a date how did the other person feel? How does your media/music make people feel? If it doesn't make people feel something, you got to go back to the drawing board!

You must tell a story that is continuous to keep people dialed into you! Your overall story has to keep people enthralled so you can elevate over the constant digital noise. You are not just seeking the consumer or your fan to listen (passive) to your music but to interact (take action) with your music. The Millennials, Generation Z and Generation Edge wish to create their own story with your song or media. You must induce them to be creative with your song so that you can acquire scale similar to Rihanna, Drake, Beyonce possess. That is the overarching goal. You must set up story telling opportunities in your media.

The currencies of the internet are time and attention! Your networks/audience/ socials are your life source. If you don't engage them, you are a dead asset. Please understand you are more than a press release that says my album/ep/single is out. You must elevate yourself above that!

What else shall you do? You have to be more creative and challenge yourself everyday.

CHAPTER 1

The Mystique is Gone

With the advent of You Tube, reality shows, social media and now live streams, there are no secrets. Creating what is called "music media" or in music parlance called "going to the studio" has been all watered down. Cheap technology has made going to the studio as easy as buying a sandwich at Subway. Apps are now available for free that allows a song/track to be created from a table or laptop while you are in your bed. It is all digital noise that can be deleted and created again for a low cost or no cost. The generation born after 1995 grew up with the rapid supply of music, which has now turned into an overabundance of music being a regular thing.

In the past there was a mystique to the process. People didn't see it created. You only heard the end result. There wasn't a day by day report. There was no watching the process as it happened. That left a mystery! Mystery is a good thing. It leaves intrigue. Intrigue makes you wonder...it makes you imagine. It forms a sense of excitement and anticipation.

The mystique now is showing as much as you can. If you are not showing (sharing) yourself and your process then people can move on to someone or something that is showing itself. Now mystique can be a negative thing. With smart phones people feel you can and should be available all the time. For all intents and purposes there is no off switch. However, I feel the one thing that has mystique still is the song writing process. Song writing is a spontaneous thing. It can come while asleep, while walking down the street or while just sitting still. Writing is a solitary endeavour. There is still a mystique to it because it is not live streamed to the world. It is quite a boring thing to see If you are watching because it is an insular activity. The result brings the song, book or script.

A mystique killer is the smart phone. It has all the tools on it for anyone to constantly be one click away from eyeballs. You can share the experience right here...right now. The cost is zero dollars! A whole generation has been groomed for no mystique. Share and share is being pushed in the marketplace always. Give it away. There is now no space for solitude. As the mantra of share, share, share is indoctrinated.

I pose one question? Do Facebook, Google or Spotify share algorithms to the public? I hope you then realize the mystique of the algorithm is its value.

Please meditate on this for a moment.

CHAPTER 2

Karaokezation of Music

At one time I worked in nightlife and there was a correlation between the club, the DJ, music and the artist. A true symbiotic relationship. They all fed each other. Not anymore due to the oversupply of music. Everyone is told go create. Keep on developing more of it and upload it to platforms. Now what that does is numb you to the product. With so much of it now it all becomes a blur. For example, at nightclubs people for the most part don't say hey that is my song and I got to dance unless it is a Future, Drake or Beyonce song. These are brands, not recording artists now. They also come from the major label system. With music being in such an abundance the importance of creating a brand will only become more important as we move forward. People need to know who made the song. This is so critical in this ecosystem which is currently being lost.

Music is more and more being reduced to being background material. It is now available in your pocket at anytime and its importance has been devalued. You can listen to it on demand. That is a process that I feel takes away from the mystique and it being special. No anticipation! Anticipation is what makes us live for what is coming next. Since there is no anticipation you now have the issue of developing the person behind the song...THE ARTIST. In this ecosystem you can know the song, but who made it? This has created a whole new situation for labels and management to deal with. Of course, technology like Shazam can tell you the name of the song which is a great thing but does the consumer dig deeper to find out the artist backstory?

That is a huge problem for artist teams. We see the effects of this daily. Here is an example, Chris Brown vs. Souljah Boy boxing match with Mike Tyson and Evander Holyfield as the corner men.

What does this have to do with music? It is an obvious publicity stunt and attention grabber. Chris Brown putting out new music isn't news anymore! It is cool but who now really cares? No anticipation. The back n forth about the boxing match smashed the internet for forty-eight hours.

In digital time that forty-eight hours is a week! Music has lost some of its shine in this current environment. It is now a tool to bring attention to things. It is a disposable thing until it isn't. I Will discuss this more later.

Software (digitization) has become the driving force during this period of systemic creativity.

Cheap software is driving the oversupply of music/media/content. The learning curve to learn a piano is totally different than to learn a software program. With digitization the emotional element has been taken out of the music. That is something that I want people to think about!

Autotune has the vocals sounding the same! The personality of the music has been lost. It is the individual that brings intangibles, software does not. One person can learn more of it than another but if you are really listening to the musical tracks that are being released it all sounds safe and similar. It has become a commodity. Once you become a commodity you become regular. As a artist you do not want to become a widget. Less risk taking is now prevalent.

Things have become more programmed. Your brand, creativity and art has to fit in the lane of sameness. But if you study history the songs (media) that have become accepted or mainstream didn't start that way. They were cutting edge, not a commodity. The goal is to be not in the box or the formula but to innovate or take a risk. The risk factor is the basis of any creative activity.

It is to challenge and bring another texture to what is already out.

To stay out of the Karaoke section and not be commoditized you have to bring a story behind the media/music. You must generate interest. You have to make people say what about that? Why did they do this? Where did it happen? That gets back to mystique. You have to leave something for people to go….hmm. Media /songs are part of the story telling process. It isn't a commodity! You as a creative person must understand this! The whole tech/media/music companies have devalued the media to the level of content. The companies want to make it about their platform/app and not about the media/music. Yet the music is the water in the pipes. You can have pipes but if there is no water the pipes are not as valuable.

The tech/software industry has tried to make it about their platforms as the key. The technology is actually the commodity not the media! Think about this...music has survived all of the technological changes. From the phonograph to streaming music has stayed resilient! The technology didn't. So, what is important in the long run? Beethoven has outlasted all the technology from his time. So please deliberate on who or what is the commodity here. Do not allow yourself to be a commodity. The technology is what is disposable not the music.

Understand music brings memories! It brings a moment. These two things are not commodities!!

Technology is a tool. Use it to make memories and moments.

CHAPTER 3

Cut Out The Unnecessary Middleman

Now you are probably asking what does this mean? Think about your media/music...how many ears it must touch to have a impact. When you make your media I assume you want the outside world beyond friends and family to experience it. You want the maximum amount of people to interact with it! How do we accomplish this? Traditionally we needed a lot of "middlemen" to touch your media so it could get to the consumer's ears. The studio owner, the radio promoter, the radio station, the video director, the video promoter, the video show, the retail promoter, distributor, but first and foremost the record label. Essentially these are the middle men. Think about it, once you finish your media all you care is to get it to people to interact with it. We needed all of those people prior to all of the technological innovation. All of those organizations were needed to get to the consumer to develop your career and your budding fan base.

The problem with all of these middle men is that there is economics involved. These costs kept so much media and artists from being discovered in this system. So many dreams were stopped from coming to life. I would make a blanket statement that anything that stops your media from going directly to the consumer is a middle man. These organizations or individuals take a cut or charge a fee. Now there is nothing wrong with this if they are providing the service they claim to do. Also, depending on where you are in your career trajectory you may not need them at that moment. This has financially and strategically crippled people in the past.

Now the blogger and social media person is a middleman telling you how much you need them and their services. They are selling fake followers, likes, views and subscribers. A lot of bloggers have very few subscribers and social media presence but yet are selling services. Be very careful In this area. Paying for a post that will likely get you little back. You can only develop your brand and artistry organically. There is no microwaving in this business. The middlemen will tell you all kinds of success stories. Always ask them about the disasters. If they act like there are no disasters just keep moving fast. They will tell you sweet stories. The best people in media have failures. Ask about the details of the disasters. This is where the truth lies. The horror stories give you the true guidance. No one wins all the time.

CHAPTER 4

Breaking A Song vs Breaking A Artist

I spent my first night with Spotify Feb 24th 2017. Yes I am late to the game. I went to search for Prohibition Artist TRAEDONYA'S! new project 4 Portraits to start to develop her in the Spotify ecosystem. We are nobodies on Spotify. My first impressions after launching our Playlist brand was that this isn't built for random discovery. I spent 6 ½ hours just looking around. I went to the artist then the song. Not the song then artist. I realized then that the process to break a artist had radically been altered. I dived in deep! It was great to go from the 40's to the present all in a click. It was fascinating to say the least. For a music head like myself it was great. The time just flew by. Then it hit me I had just went to all of the artist that I could think of. What about all of the emerging /unknown and new artists? Then I was like wow!

How do you get through this logjam of music? So now I knew the game had changed. I really saw now that you really must stay on this one portal to break your music through! There are no real gatekeepers like before. Of course you have the playlists curators of Spotify and all of the user generated playlist developers. But the big story is the Spotify algorithm. The algorithm is king. It is too much music now. The algorithm allows all this music to be recognized. There is simply not enough time to listen to this constant overload of music. It never stops. What this Spotify or streaming culture means is that for all intents and purposes there is no old music. It is just music waiting to be discovered by people. If someone discovers one song, they may go through the artist whole catalogue! This is a bonus of huge proportions. This is now a game of song development, not artist development. This has an overwhelming effect on what is called the ANR process in the music economy business design. You are now focused on the song. The lyrics of it.

The backing track, mood and feel of the song. Genres are not your only way of thinking about the song. You have to break a song down. What instrument is focused in it? What is the story of the lyric? I feel song writing has become more and more important in the streaming era. Production can be automated. You can buy software today and make music tomorrow. You don't have to know how to play instruments. In my opinion, technological development has made the song (lyrics) the crux with context and not genre being the driving force in song marketing. Lyric sheets, lyric videos and lyric readings are a very critical promotional tool. Dive in to the lyrics.

Streaming will cut out many of the industry middlemen. Your budgets can now be so much smaller if you engage the Spotify platform. As I write, Spotify(streaming) is becoming more dominant. Spotify has just reported over 100 million subscribers with over 50 million paying.

There are of course other platforms like Apple Music, Deezer, Tidal, Google play/You Tube and Pandora but for our purposes here we are discussing Spotify. Streaming has a very large effect on how a song develops now. The song goes global first! Then it comes back local. These platforms are global not local. So your song can become a global record without all of the global infrastructure cost of the past. For someone like me, who relocated to another country and dived into the music culture in the U.K, this is mind blowing. There is absolutely no cost to sit in front of your computer, tablet or phone. The business has shifted to who has the time to be on the platforms. I realize the strategic mistake I made not diving in. I dived into social media and PR.

But now I get it. I was aware of streaming but missed the boat. The streaming sites are for song, not artist development. I remember artist development and have to adjust to this new conceptual way. The artist is secondary in the streaming ecosystem. Now you must separate the jobs of song and artist development. They used to be together but not now. I am processing this myself. I am happy that I know this now. This will stop future confusion. This has officially shifted my internal business model asap. It has altered so much. I am in scramble alert to upgrade our internal operations. With all of this going on here is a stat to mull over…there are over 2 billion playlists just on Spotify. Spotify is the big boy, so we use them as a proxy. Here are billions of opportunities for your song to be programmed. Essentially you are in the "song competition business". I know it is hard to maybe picture this but please do. The big competition is for the Spotify editorial playlists. Those are the ones the major labels have a stranglehold on. The large branded ones such as Pitchfork are next in the food chain. There is about an estimated 5000 of those playlist.

Your internal squad has to dive in deep here. Take the time and do it. It doesn't cost anything but time. Time is the main currency on the internet. That is the conundrum. The key to Spotify is your fan base or lack of. Your fans on Spotify are the first people who can get the song out and about. You need them to add it to their personal playlists. Follow you on Spotify. The artist pages are the global headquarters! It is where people will go to find you. Your Spotify link needs to be in all of your social media, website and press. You need to be pushing that link. Call yourself the link pusher! All of this is free. So hypothetically you can craft a big record for zero dollars. That is a mind blowing concept. The tech/music companies do not care what song "blows up". In fact they prefer an unknown song to win so they can publicize the story. Now you should spend time to figure out the various platforms with a bullseye on Spotify. Do your homework. There isn't a gatekeeper stopping you from learning to work these platforms for your benefit.

CHAPTER 5

References and Relationships

Today is Feb 27th 2017 and while walking this chapter came into my head. I am in the process of ramping up DJ & club promotion for the 4 Portraits Project. I wasn't going to do any DJ Promo because that area has changed so much. A lot of the contacts are not in business anymore. So I didn't know where to start! After I went through my notes and researched 2/3 of my contacts were gone. I was blown away. The technological changes had just brushed away so many who provided solid services. The whole concept of breaking a record has been altered permanently. At that point I was starting from scratch in so many ways. I had to dispose of twenty years. Alot of relationships had evaporated. The fun was gone. I had essentially was back at square one after 20 years. It was very disheartening.

The more current attitude is music discovery which the tech/music companies are great at. But breaking a record involves the artist. It connects the artist to the song. The artist rides along with the song. The fans can like a song but just focus on the song because it is added to the playlist.

That is a win for the song but the artist is still a mystery. The artist needs to be truly connected to the song so their brand can start to develop. The brand is where so much revenue is derived from now. The music opens the door, but it isn't the end game like it was in the past.

Now back to what we are discussing...oh yes references & relationships. So I decided to go back old school and work the record again. This has been lost a bit in the tech/music world. The breaking of the record allows the discussion of the song/track. Intimate information which can be generated and you learn something from credible professional ears. Of course fans will give you feedback through data but to be able to talk about the music is a priceless experience. That can start a relationship in the inner game. You can get referrals to bigger situations. This is the behind the scenes movements that the tech/music world is not good at yet. Yes your media can move around with ease but the relationship offers a intangible unknown. That is the core value of the relationship. It can continue and evolve wherever each of you goes. The relationship goes on and on when that initial moment is over.

This is our first project to retail since 2011 and since that time I have noticed a shift. The new media ecosystem is built on content not media. Content can be anything. So now your music/video is content, not media in this current ecosystem. When you are sending out your project it is just one of the thousands a media outlet/DJ or distributor is getting weekly or daily. One of the organizations I didn't have a relationship with told me they were getting 1500 new songs a week to go through. How do they do this? Think about that. There is not enough time in the day let alone a week to go through it all. I truly saw right there that this is a different business! How do we really get through in this flood of music, media and content? Before you had to reach people on the phone but now that is a rare occurrence. All you get is voice mails now. People don't wish to talk on the phone now. It is just send the mp3 and that's it. People don't want to even start a dialogue. It makes sense though because so many people just drop in and out of the business now. So, I assume people ask why bother to talk? Without that relationship you can't get quality references! The references are priceless because you don't know what door it can open. I got a reference yesterday that may allow me to speak at a college to students about the media industry. If I hadn't gotten on the phone to forge a relationship and start a dialogue that does not happen.

Luckily, I had some relationships that allowed me to get the song heard by some tastemakers and get critical feedback in 24 hours so I could make critical decisions that are strategic and financial. We know what we have to do now. Being able to have a conversation and get inside information allowed me to make better decisions. This is the type of information that data can't tell you. We now know what song the industry types will support and what tactics to utilize. The data can't give you all this information. I am just saying not to reject relationships.

For the record I had not spoken to these organizations in 6-7 years, but it didn't matter. There was the prior connection which now can't be replicated. Another instance where the past relationship came in handy was video promotion. In the past I did my own nationwide video promotion with a marketing company filling in the blanks where I didn't have coverage. During the promotion we toured through 52 cities in North America/Canada learning the intangibles that you can only learn if you are in those cities and regions. This is what the major labels have over independents. They know the ground usually better than we do. This isn't the case as much anymore but is the general consensus. Even now 6-7 years later the past relationships will allow us to cut through so much red tape. We have the knowledge of what cities to go to and ones to fly over unless we get a very good reason to go. We use the technology and the old relationships.

The video Industry is less personal now and you are dependent on the online outlets. So much of how we acquired rotation for our video was being able to make a phone call. At the end of the day you want to be a priority. Videos(music) are not the big event they were, due to the supply of so many of them and the fact that they can be made for all intents and purposes for nothing.

The information I was able to ascertain helped us immensely. This saved so much time in our marketing plan. I saw that without the old connections it would have cost us time and capital.

Also I saw so much of my marketing plan wasn't relevant anymore. It is scary but this is what we do. You have to stay relevant and current. It isn't about being popular necessarily now but being relevant to your base and build out. So go out and talk to people. The human touch will allow you to one up others. With the flood of content and many more outlets available the game has shifted back to one of relationships and references I feel. These two things can't be procured with data! I am saying do not be one dimensional in how you operate.

CHAPTER 6

Music As A Branding Tool

In 2017 in my opinion music is not in a distinctive category anymore. It is lumped in with all media and content. This started with the genesis of the iTunes platform. All categories of entertainment from film, tv, gaming, books and music are lumped together. With the fact that talent is not the driving force in media anymore, music has become commoditized. It has fallen from the exalted perch of a craft or art. It is now made from a technological base. You press a button and you get an instrument. You do not need an instrumentalist to play the part.

You can be the whole band or ensemble now yet know very little about instruments.

I am leading to the point of this chapter which is now music is something you do. You do it for a hobby. You do it because it is cool. You do it to relax. All these reasons are fine. I am just prefacing the landscape. In this ecosystem people are making a record because they have a following or are a brand. They have a ready made audience that will consume what they offer.

So, hey why not put out a record? It is totally economically sensible. It is very cheap and easy to do. It is easier to make a recording than to do a commercial. You can bring attention to a product or a service very economically. An example of this is reality show stars (brands) putting out music. You figure they have hundreds of thousands and in some cases millions of people watching them. The audience will definitely give it a chance. It is very cheap to promote. It has a symbiotic relationship with the star or brand! In this streaming landscape which is driven by singles not albums this is even more compelling. Albums take vision, time, song writing and production. That is a lot of work. But in this new media ecosystem you can just release one recording as a brand because people don't even have to buy it anymore. They can consume and add it to a playlist. IT IS A BRAND EXTENSION NOT A RECORDING ANYMORE. You can record a song on your laptop and immediately upload it. It is not necessarily going to a distributor for sale or official stream. It can just go up on You Tube and be tweeted out to followers/subscribers.

Lets expand on this using the current top tv show Empire. First of all I have never watched it but of course I know the show because of the star power of Taraji Henson and Terrence Howard. I started noticing music being featured from the show on music and lifestyle blogs I subscribe to.

I said to myself what is this? I mean think about it, there was no lead up to it.

It just comes out via the show. That is genius. No promotional costs. It is bundled with the show and the stars who are doing the records. Now the music is merchandise from the show. The great part is that you don't have to promote and market extensively. I assume it is woven into the show. It doesn't need introducing. All it needs is to be available once it is shown on the show! It is a brand extension piece. Then when the stars get interviewed about the show the song can piggyback and vice versa. Music is now a commoditized/brand extension.

CHAPTER 7

PR Has Been Replaced By Social Media Trolling

In 2017 we are all in the attention business whether you know it or not. The music is part of the campaign but not like before. In hip hop "the beef" has always been part of the competitive spirit of that genre. In 2017 it is the total campaign and the music is the conduit. Lets discuss two situations where music is the conduit and where the beef was the major attention on the internet for 72-96 hours. In the digital world that is longer than the 3 – 4 days. The object of any and all businesses is to go viral or create an old-fashioned stir! It happens exponentially and can just appear out of the blue. It just spreads out into peoples newsfeeds and then it is the talk of the globe forget the town.

Case 1 – Souljah Boy vs Chris Brown I watched it evolve in a matter of 24 hours. They started arguing on I believe Twitter and then it escalated to Instagram video and then 50 Cent got involved with Mike Tyson and Floyd Mayweather. All these people have millions of followers! Souljah Boy talked about Chris Brown's daughter! From there Chris said keep my daughter's name out of your mouth via Instagram video. Then the next thing they are having a boxing match to settle the beef. From there I see 50 Cent on Instagram picked up by blogs showing him giggling while talking about the fight with Mike Tyson on speaker phone. Tyson is in 1988 mode while talking about the proposed fight. 1988 mode means a young and wild Mike Tyson. He then decides he will train Chris Brown after it apparently came out that Floyd Mayweather will train Souljah Boy. So, you have these five huge brands with large social followings involved! This thing has now gotten picked up around the world! I saw it on Nigerian, South African and Kenyan blogs. I was like wow...all in 48 hours. It just snowballed into a thing. Twitter and Instagram wash, rinse and repeat! I was like wow this is what it has come to. It became a life of its own. I mean who really wants to see such a fight when you think about it! The hype alone just subdued any sensibilities about this. Then on top of that Mike Tyson released a rap song. I started laughing. I mean it wasn't as bad as I thought it would be. It wasn't a bad idea. A music video came out and went viral on the internet.

I realized that things can't be serious. I was just shaking my head! Then I see Souljah Boy drops his new mix tape. I said this is the new marketing/PR campaign launch to bring attention to what you are doing. Then I see that Chris Brown is announcing an arena tour! I was like huh... ok that was the reason. A PR campaign in the traditional sense can not get you that kind of "exponential awareness". The web is built for 0-200 M.P.H in 4 seconds. It is not a slow groove thing. Not organic at all. You need trolling, gimmicks and over the top behaviour with Influencers or brands that can help push it out all over people's feeds. With people checking there newsfeeds on social media you need something that is interesting to cut through the over abundance of media/content.

Case 2 – Nicki Minaj vs. Remy Ma. Now this was an old fashion rap beef. But again, this just happens to come out right when Remy Ma and Fat Joe released their new album. They locked down the internet for a week.

Remy put out a diss record on Nicki and it got 2.4 million streams on Soundcloud in 24 hours. It went viral and crossed over into mainstream press. It also was post-Grammy time, so it brought more attention to her and Fat Joe's new album. Her next step was to go on Wendy Williams show wearing black as if she was going to a funeral for Nicki. The lyrics were broken down and analysed by bloggers and fans. Nicki was silent throughout this time. A week later Nicki released her diss record with Lil Wayne and Drake. Now that is a lot of Juice. The song went viral in a few hours and then I saw it on hip hop and lifestyle blogs everywhere. You can't buy this type of PR.

The Twitter verse and Instagram went crazy. Nicki's lyrics were analysed and discussed. As I write, this is happening fast and building exponentially. These are the two biggest female rappers around now. They both have their online coalitions of millions who will cause the story to spread just by "pressing send". I feel a traditional PR campaign doesn't work in this new media hyper flow of information/news. You need to entertain, get people's attention, get them laughing and then telling their friends about what you are doing. The slow death of what is called PR has been sped up. You have to figure out ways to capture peoples attention! A core part of what you do will be in the attention business. If you don't get their attention some one else will. The old playbook of " my new single is out"..."my new Ep is out" is antiquated. No one cares. It is just too much dang music out now. I want you to think like a consumer here. All of this choice of media now. Yet the 24 hour day has not changed. You still have to work, sleep and do all of the other daily activities we do as humans. So please tell me how will you get peoples attention to notice your creative output. Please deliberate and meditate on this. Stop reading and meditate.

CHAPTER 8

Mainstream is Dead in 2017

Every new brand (music artist) must identify their own niche in order to build out a business. This is what I have theorized due to the digital ecosystem which has taken over our world. Social media has taken its toll on the mainstream. People identify with their own channels now. The mass market has taken a step back. IN ORDER TO GROW YOUR BUSINESS AND BRAND YOU HAVE TO OWN YOUR INITIAL NICHE. WHO CAN GIVE YOU AND YOUR MEDIA THE INITIAL SUPPORT SYSTEM. So instead of going after everyone you must define yourself and define your market. This way you can then put your limited resources to their best use. In the past you had to reach everyone so you could get your audience. The only tools available were the mass market strategies which were expensive and shut out people from following through. Now you can find your niche on social media and go after that base to develop your business. This is the most economical intelligent way to go. You can find peoples preferences and interest on social media.

Get use to the term "silo marketing". So for example you can just spend your time on one platform. Since Spotify has the largest subscriber base of 100 million, it makes the most sense to focus on this silo. So if you and your team know your identity which allows you to know your niche you then can say let's develop our base and throw the kitchen sink at it. You keep releasing music consistently along with strategic content segments. In this digital era you must "feed your audience" because if you don't someone else will fill that vacuum. You should become a integral part of the Spotify ecosystem! You develop playlists and market those playlists through your ecosystem. You follow other artists. Use your social media as a delivery system. Again please choose the social media portal that fits your personality the best! The one you feel most comfortable with and develop your profile there. You can't be everywhere now. There is not enough time in the day. That is a mainstream tactic! If you cultivate your niche your niche will then cultivate you. You have to understand that the mainstream is dead. The world has evolved to a niche marketplace and the truth is you do not have the time to cover all of the bases. You have to know where you fit in. This is very critical to your potential success. You can only do this by doing! You can't do this in theory.

Do not look at the mainstream artists Beyonce, Lady Gaga and Britney Spears as doing what you do. They come from a different ecosphere. The digital ecosystem is built on finding where you fit. That is where you put your energy and time. The new media world allows everyone to hear, see and read exactly what they want to. However, now this has other very serious effects. For our purposes we want to amplify the effects of this digital ecosystem based on niche marketing not mass marketing.

CASE STUDY For example, if you are a techno artist you can find out through the search on Spotify and plug into that community. Also, who are the editors/curators for them? This can be done by you and your team. As I already discussed you don't need an intermediary like in the past. Knowing your niche empowers you to take ownership of your career and trajectory of your budding career.

In closing, the main thing is to dive in deep! Don't wait dive in. There is no more "Wizard of Oz". You are your own wizard.

CHAPTER 9

The Global Record

In this new media/Spotify ecosystem an artist can have a global hit song without a global Infrastructure. Prior to this you had to release the record in every territory or get licensing deals in territories. Now you can have a global audience by just "pressing send". For example, if you have a song that has 5 million streams it is broken down by territory, in my case the USA market. You can now literally be travelling in 6 months of starting your career to paid shows without ever doing any promo work in the market. Your song can be moving around via playlists and the Spotify algorithm without you doing all the heavy lifting on the record by yourself.

Prior to this you needed a label and its various teams to move that song around. The song is going into the music lover's sphere without all the middlemen that was needed in the past. You do not need that global infrastructure now to have a global hit. You need to amplify what we have been discussing throughout this narrative. The digital ecosystem is built to grow a global record not a local record! You have to think in a global mindset now. Your song may not work in your city but it can work elsewhere. So you have to be aware and on top of your game. Be focused. Don't worry about your friends, your neighbourhood, your city, your region or even your country! The digital ecosystem is a global village. Therefore your media/content and music is global. This has opened all possibilities for your eventual brand. So embrace the global village of music lovers in your initial niche.

CHAPTER 10

The Store Don't Close

We now live in a 24/7 news cycle. An on-demand world. So that goes for your media/music/content and most importantly your brand. Just because where you are is night time and people are sleeping doesn't mean anything in the digital space has stopped churning. It just follows the sun. So when the sun rises again business commences again. People are streaming, buying, listening and watching videos somewhere while you are sleeping. Someone can be checking your profile when you are sleeping. You and your brand are open for business around the clock.

Now this means there is always an opportunity for someone to engage with you digitally. So, your social media profiles, your website(HQ) of your brand are always available. Your music/videos are available for someone to bump into. If you are a soul singer people can find you via that search and click around to check you out! YOU ARE NEVER CLOSED FOR BUSINESS! You need to incorporate this thinking in your business philosophy. It sets a tone that once you embrace it and it sinks in it should make you look at what you are doing in a different light. "THE STORE DON'T CLOSE"! You are open for business 24/7. You must incorporate this into your business design.

For me I don't care where it happens, as long as it is happening. The problem starts if nothing is happening nowhere! So, embrace this mindset. It will change your life as well as your business.

CHAPTER 11

The Store Is In Your Pocket

The iPhone along with iTunes changed the concept of going to the store for music and as time moved on the other key media categories. Then you add in Amazon for books and we have lived through the media revolution not truly realizing it. Historians will eventually discuss this period as the transition from physical media to digital media.

I want to say that we have to truly understand the thing we carry around with us everyday. That thing being the smart phone. I come from the age VHS, DVD and CD when you had physical media. We now are in the total digitization of media yet I still didn't totally grasp the thing in my pocket called a phone. I have called them a P.E.D(Personal Entertainment Device) but now going one step further and calling it a P.R.S.D(Personal Retail Store Device). As we are in the music/media/content business and do all our marketing, PR with this device. We know that you can go to all of the retail platforms yet I have never seen this broken down bare bones regarding the smart phone. That device in your pocket can go directly to Spotify, iTunes, Apple Music, Google Play, YouTube, Shazam, Napster, Deezer and Pandora. These are the stores or apps where so much monetization of musical media stem from. It is right there in someone's pocket. No one has to get in their car to go to a retail store. They do not have to wait to go experience, stream or purchase your song if they heard it. Conceptually what does this mean? To me it means that your media and brand can be sold or consumed at anytime!

You must get that person to go in their pocket and pull your music up. It means from here consider the smart phone a RETAIL STORE! It is a RETAIL DEVICE! It is not just for social media, trolling, watching videos and research but it is a monetization device. You are able to make money at any time as well as have a meeting about yourself. I still hear artists say at concerts and live events "IN STORES NOW". The proper way now is "IT IS IN YOUR PHONE RIGHT NOW" by saying it the new way, people can go right to your music in the moment. "In stores" seems like they have to leave and go elsewhere. There is no wait now! We must conceptually realize that by stating the old way you are putting up a roadblock to monetization. Lets all stop this! If you are on stage you pull out your phone and say to the audience it is in your phone right now!

Let's all of us go to my song I just sang to you right now and book mark my Spotify page. Save my single to your playlist. Share with your friends right now. Tell them that you are at my show and just heard it live! Go stream it now and put it on your personal playlist. Now stop and reflect on what you just read! Now you have everyone's attention from the stage. That is the powerful drug of attention! This device makes you on demand wherever and, however. So utilize this P.R.S.D in your pocket the way it is supposed to be used. Think about this now...what is between your media and the fan now? There is really nothing! You just need their attention!

That is the crux! This is why I keep repeating that your are in the ATTENTION BUSINESS! You are in the TIME BUSINESS! There is no intermediary! What are your challenges now? You need to cut down all of the mental roadblocks now. Your media/content for monetization is "ONE CLICK AWAY" now meditate on that! Stop and think what that means. You need to have your links to all of the key retail stores every where your brand is! If now with your phone you are a link and a click away from monetization how does this simplify what you are truly doing? You now can cut out all of the unnecessary noise! You cut out all of the unnecessary cost of doing business. This also empowers you to realize you are in business. You are not just doing this for a hobby. YOU ARE ALWAYS ONE CLICK AWAY FROM YOUR MEDIA BEING MONETIZED.

You have to look at every single phone as your retail store! YOUR STORE FRONT IS IN EVERY SINGLE PHONE! Now please meditate on that! If you could get 100 million peoples attention to go to their phone and go to your link to your store fronts on Spotify and iTunes/Apple Music what would this do for your career? We see this every year now on Super Bowl Sunday! Lady Gaga worked for free at halftime as the Super Bowl performer. People were sitting on the couch with their phone near them and went to her stores right then in the moment. Now I hope you are truly understanding

"THE STORE IS IN YOUR POCKET". So that you get it...every time you have a audience whether online (live stream concert, press event or chat) or you are performing live you can send people to your store in the moment. No delays! Like the song says...RIGHT HERE RIGHT NOW! Look at your phone now! Stare at it. Grasp the power it gives you if you truly use it how it can and should be used. Amazing right?

THE FINAL FRONTIER in closing, life is simple as a professional media producer. The online world I hope will give you the courage to follow your dream! To identify what you want to do. That can be scary because now you can see the "BLUE OCEAN". It is all clear. Now you alter your days to accomplish your aim and make the proper choices and allow you to focus your attention on what is necessary and remove all the unnecessary people, places and things. You can do anything you want just not everything.

I want to say mind is "cleaning out the basement" while going through this process. For me to stay relevant and be in this business I will have to keep transforming myself. This is just a beginning I can see. I hope by reading this you find a direction if you didn't have one prior.

Please attack It with all the necessary urgency. In this evolving ecosystem you only learn by being in the game. Get off the side lines. As I learned playing blackjack on my stoop as 13-year-old

"SCARED MONEY DON'T MAKE NO MONEY".

I wrote this narrative because so many of the strategies and tools I had etched in stone didn't work as well anymore. They still cost capital but were not as effective. The tech/music portals along with social media platforms have literally made it possible for someone to say why not do it. All the things I discussed I had to evolve to from Narrative one to now as I release Our first project by vocalist TRAEDONYA! Aka "The Bride of New Funk Hipopera" in Six years. Hence, I made a lot of errors that in the past would have been detrimental to what we are doing. But due to everything I discussed you do get a do over! That is what is so great! In the past there was no comeback unless you got more capital. Now you can refine everything along the way and stay in the game. It all media/content now. Hence, we are just telling stories and having a great time embracing opportunity. This is an exciting and challenging time because through all of this I want to end this by saying we are all trying to get each other's attention! Hence, the first business you are in is what? THE ATTENTION BUSINESS. Much success chasing attention. Cheers A.K Smith-Ford May 2nd 2017

EPILOGUE

My first narrative was called Live Digital or Be Irrelevant! That narrative can be found at https://www.akcidentalwriter.com and all the top retailers. I have come up with a definition of what living digital means: Be ready and on constant alert for the abundance of digital opportunities for your brand online in what the technologist term the "network economy". This time we are living in is similar to the mid 1800's to the 1930's when the industrial revolution was in full rage and massive changes to the economy were taking place. What I have learned is that I have opportunities anytime and everyday if I am dialed into what is going on in the moment. The old music economy was purely about who you know. It was very insular and capital intensive. It is less of that now due to the digital network economy. The music business has been the guinea pig for this new economy we all shall be navigating in. DUE TO THIS SOCIETY AS A WHOLE IS IN THE MUSIC BUSINESS WITHOUT BEING TOLD THEY ARE. Things change constantly now and music has always evolved quickly in the past. We live in the trend economy which is the basis of the viral economy. Who is trendier than the professional recording artist…maybe a fashionista? I would put music number one. Music made the video crucial in society. In all the tech literature it is touting video as a saviour to marketing and how important it is. What about live streaming? Who is about the live show more than the recording artist? Aren't the tech companies touting live streaming. I was going to leave the music business but after seeing the world correctly and seeing that all digital behemoths are diving in and are finally paying via licensing deals I stood in it. The digital companies built their companies without paying rights holders for many years. This has assisted in turning music into a commodity over the past 15 years. The playlist has devalued the standalone album by the artist. The deeper purpose of an album was a channel for the professional recording artist to create their masterpiece and develop a solid brand to make a living from. The playlist is just a collection of songs. I am not griping here just explaining. Enough of me on my soap box…lol.

Music is perfect for the network economy! All we do is think of creating something. We spend our time on how we get noticed. We are the originators of the attention economy. The software that is available to make all these cheap digital creations that feeds the algorithms of the technological giants are everywhere. It is all loaded on computers or downloadable from the app store. What has been the biggest hustle in the last 7 years…Uber which is a glorified taxi service.

People use their own cars and get the money last. That is the most amazing hustle. It is an app which can essentially appear anywhere. That is the beauty of the network economy! Global opportunities are available 24/7 around the clock if you are grinding hard. I am looking at this in many dimensions now. I am no expert because things change too quick now. The information is constantly being updated and adjusted. Unless you keep current how can you be an expert in this era? The information is constantly being disrupted. THE IDEA OF AN EXPERT MUST BE REEVALUATED GOING FORWARD AS WE MOVE DEEPER INTO THE 2020'S. It is imperative to understand that aspect of the network economy. The opportunities and information is always in a constant mutational state. Don't despair because there is something else always coming! You are never out of the game. It is your responsibility to be always prepping for the next opportunity. Always sniffing around for it. What this means to me on a personal level is that I always have the opportunity to alter my life in the moment and definitely in the future. I am taking control of my existence; something most people do not have the opportunity to do.

In the network economy you must have ownership of what you do. Ownership is the key!

Ownership means you have a stake in your fate or destiny, and you are not just a cog. I am saying this from a very personal perspective as I have just been downsized from my corporate part time gig. Living in the NYC real estate market you always must keep a job for rent...lol. For me that is very powerful and compelling thing that I had to understand so I could shift my thoughts from despair to being joyful and optimistic. That is the compelling thing the technologist have done for us if you embrace what the network economy truly means which is endless opportunities. You can't sit and wait for things anymore! You must be pitching and releasing your content/media/services. You must have a developed brand to be noticed. The downside of all this opportunity is that the whole globe is competing now. I see we are and will be living in a global hunger games. No more protections. There will be billions in pursuit potentially. For me the future is the present moment we are in. Everyone is consistently working now. You better like what you do because if you don't it will be long miserable days that seem like they never end. My days go my fast because I spend my whole day in constant pursuit of opportunities and due to my foundation in independent music along with my marketing background I am perfectly ready for this era we are embarking on. In this next chapter, I will be living digital all the way. Living digital is about I can be anywhere with internet/wi fi connection available and work. In the pages ahead I hope to inspire others to realize that living digital will be a regular way of living in the 2020's. Living digital is about betting on yourself and your concepts or ideas. Living digital is being in the state of constant "UNLEARNING". Unlearning I discuss in my first narrative Live Digital or Be Irrelevant.

Living digital is understanding the only way to strive and survive will be to take a different outlook on life and transform your thought patterns. Living digital is realizing that time is your ultimate currency and what you do with it will define your future destination. Things do not wait in this era I implore you to not hesitate in this network economy. The ability to make quick executive decisions that are durable in your daily life will be a very vital skillset! Please invest in a book or course in critical and strategic thinking.

    A.K Smith-Ford Sept 25th 2019 7:08pm

PART 3

POST COVID-19 (P.C) OUTBREAK EXTENSION – VALIDATION OF TRENDS/CONCEPT/VISION.

August 2nd 2020 5:58pm on the waterfront.

Reprogramming of the humans by the powers that be has really begun. The powers that be do not need the humans for mass physical labor anymore, they are needed for a new kind of mass labor now. So, what do you do with all of them going forward? You get rid of or you reprogram them.

DIGITAL BILL OF RIGHTS

- Your future success lies in the unknown. You better accept and embrace that fact.
- The digital world is a rollercoaster…get used to it.
- Remove the F word failure from your narrative! It is all experience now.
- Stop thinking in terms of safety and security. The only safety net is applying the change coming at you in abundance.
- You are in the time business,
- You are in the attention business.
- Opportunities are available for you every day to succeed. Start noticing.
- Cultivate your brand!
- You will have to share yourself to your network and or audience.
- People buy why you do not what you do.
- Create a more fluid story for your brand.
- This is the age of action not in action.
- FEAR IS TOO BE UNINSTALLED FROM YOUR PERSONAL ALGORITHM.
- The digital store doesn't close. This means neither does your brand.
- The only arbitrators of your work are the consumer or your network.
- POINT ALL OF YOUR LIMITED ASSETS TO THE DIGITAL DIASPORA AND UTILIZE THE PRINCIPLES IN THIS NARRATIVE.
- Interaction and engagement not PR are what matters now. Please learn the difference.
- Digital will allow you to increase your probability of economic success.
- DIGITAL MAKES EVERYTHING A WORK IN PROGRESS.
- THE IDEA OF NORMAL HAS TO BE UNINSTALLED FROM YOUR PERSONAL ALGORITHM.
- Live digital or surely become irrelevant.

By following all of the above you will then be on your way to #DIGITALCITIZENSHIP

FOREWARNED

I wish to say that I am now a professional "digital social observer theorist". At the heart of it all I am a philosopher. The post corona future time period will be one of heightened change. It shall be one of challenging yourself to do things constantly that were not done by you prior. How to rethink or think anew. I CALL IT "TOSS THE PLAYBOOK SYNDROME". It will be a time of not incremental behavior but one of exponential behavior due to the underlying digital component to the economy. Let's look at the definition of both:

Incremental – Relating to or denoting an increase or addition, especially one of a fixed scale.

Exponential - (Of an increase) becoming more and more rapid especially by large amounts.

A job is considered an incremental improvement which for me always said I would have a limited existence unless I made changes in my life; but more important how I saw life. I saw how the cards were dealt to me and they were stacked against me if I wanted something different. I have been in pursuit for something totally different since tenth grade. In this digital post corona environment life will be much more abrupt and exponential so I have decided to go all in on my observations. #PRACTICEWHATYOUPREACH. The summer of 2020 I am finally relaunching my business after a four-year journey. A multimedia entrepreneur with an emphasis on the cultural narrative. This is my life now and I will not go back to the incremental lifestyle. I realize I live in a 24/7 around the clock world now and what that means. I like to say "The store doesn't close". In E commerce the store is always open. Inclement weather doesn't stop the digital business; in fact, it is a plus! People are sitting around bored and available via there plethora of devices.

In our exponential present future, the key to making progress will be to ask the right questions. In school we are taught for the most part to look for answers. Rote memorization has been replaced by Google. I will go back to philosophy class during my "long weekend" in college, I left early because it was not for me. I recall the professor would say I am looking for some answers to challenge us. I still use that in conversations, however now for me the question not the answer is my focus. I always attempt to go nonlinear in my question pattern to challenge the assumptions. IN THE DIGITAL WORLD ONE SIZE DOES NOT FIT ALL. It is all based on personal choice and whether one participates. In this age people can get what they want and when they want it. No real limits or scarcity. The principle of scarcity doesn't exist online. As long as you have access you are good and in the game. The keys in the post corona living lifestyle everything will be about heightened dehumanization, your creativity, collaborative skills, critical thinking, problem solving and specialized innovation skill sets based on your uniqueness. That list will allow you the best chance to do exponential activities. An example of this is the energy problem. Think about this we have the greatest source of energy in the sun. In theory I read something somewhere in an hour more energy hits the earth surface via the sun than all of the fossil fuels in a year. Please pause and think about that for a moment. THE LIMITS ARE UP TO THE INDIVIDUAL. The limits will be based on the questions you ask yourself. As you question more you will keep coming up with more questions which is your fuel in the digital world so you can then hopefully innovate something but more importantly transform it.

Exponential technology(thoughts) allows small groups or individuals to do things that only governments or billion-dollar corporations did in the past. I am an example of this due to the fact I created my first mobile game app and will make a drastic exponential change to my daily lifestyle in the very immediate future. The game is something I would not have fathomed in 2015. I am a living breathing example of what I am saying here in these pages.

Scarcity is now a contextual thing if we refit our personal viewpoint. In order to do that we will have to overcome the HUMAN CONDITIONS of being a cynic, pessimist and other "negative fuels that are out and about lurking every day. We forget every day especially here in America you have choices and or options. You have the option to ingest negative fuel or positive fuel. That is a choice. The bulk of people live in their linear brain not their nonlinear brain. That nonlinear brain is the one that seeks exponential possibilities. I am stating here you will have to retrain your brain as we move deeper into the 2020's! You will have to challenge yourself constantly. No government office can help you on this and there is no "diet pill" for that. We are taught to feed our limitations. We are programmed to scrap our imagination especially as we get older. #SCRAPTHOSEDREAMS. The key for me is to look at something and challenge myself to see what isn't there. Please stop and meditate on that statement.

In this post corona digital economy time is your most precious resource! Money is not. Each of us is allotted 24 hours from the richest financially to the poorest. What we do with this precious resource in my eyes is the ultimate equalizer and will determine our quality of life. The measure we should focus on in the immediate future is not dollars, euros or yen; the measure is the time it takes to acquire those currencies. I REPEAT IN THE DIGITAL SPACE TIME IS YOUR ULTIMATE RESOURCE. Please change your focus from here. Stop reading and do a deep think.

In the old-world catering to the rich was the main element to succeed. In the post corona time, the needs of the masses will be your meal ticket to another life. It is another choice/option due to things like microfinance/mobile technology that gives the huge capability to create more intraclass opportunities that are not only for the wealthy or big corporation. Due to this technology we will add billions of consumers in the 2020's. On the defensive side of the ball this means we are adding billions of potential competitors. On the offensive side of the ball we are adding billions of opportunities! Opportunities that in theory are available 24/7. You better be preparing yourself for this tsunami. That is my future as well as yours. In my eyes it is sobering yet a very large opportunity to make exponential change consistently to your future.

I have come up with two formulas that I will use here to keep us clear on what we have to do:

Formula one -

    Product(service) + specialized innovation + time saved = PROSPERITY

Formula two -

    Time + idea creation + concentration in the moment + earned attention of others + media attention = PROSPERITY

Conclusion: If you are reading this then you realize that a change is needed in how you are living. What I really am saying is how you are thinking or see the world. The age of viewing a college diploma as a proxy for ability is over, that is based on antiquated industrial age ideas. Going for the diploma still is critical I feel, but not as that guarantee that it was in the past. You will have to show what you do going forward. If you have young kids right now it something to think about very deeply.

My overarching message is to view the world via a different lens and utilize your time in a different manner. Let's move on.

    A.K Smith-Ford 6/12/20 8:35pm

OBSERVATION ONE

The human is a biohazard in the 2020 P.C (Post Corona)

In this post corona period, the human is a pestilence. We now live in a quote un quote infectious environment. This means stay away. Social distancing and isolation are saying keep away from each other. Who will benefit? I say big tech of course and people/businesses positioning themselves that take advantage of these trends. Please position yourself accordingly. The post corona period will speed up tech related innovations that involve not touching or as I like to say not being human or being physical. THE NATURE OF FAMEDOM AND FANDOM HAS BEEN COMPLETELY REDESIGNED DURING THE PANDEMIC. This has impacted how we brand ourselves, which is essential to all of our future.

Everyone has become D.I.Y due to the pandemic. Everyone now is doing what independent record companies have always done, we figured it out! This will continue and is a mindset that will be prized. THE NEW STAR QUALITY IS SHOWING YOUR HUMANITY! Doing the human things not the mystical things. Famous actors showed themselves without the "Hollywood machinery" on social showing, hey I am just like you. Prior to this "stars" were removed from us. Stars had mystique or otherness. Since the social media era started little by little the "Hollywood effect" has been dismantled. The corona pandemic has severely wounded the mystique of a hundred years of developing that whole system. Everyone no matter what level was sequestered at home, this displayed we are all the same no matter what level. I am stating here the star system set up in the 1920's - 1930's has been retired for the most part. I am including big music companies who used the old system also. The major label music system for me is dead. It is for the most part data and technology with very little to do with music talent. Another example is the movie premiere which during the pandemic with movie theatres closed companies had to make quick adjustments. An example of this was Trolls and The Scooby movies which were utilized as guinea pigs to test the idea of video on demand premieres at the height of the quarantine in late spring 2020. The whole idea of it has to go to a movie theatre (human gathering) is definitely being challenged. Did the pandemic stop media companies from premiering? Yes and no. A lot of the tentpole movies were pushed back. However, it did show the future. Some movies were sold to streaming apps like Apple and Netflix. It said to me you better be asking how can you make whatever you are doing increasingly virtual or less exposed to human gathering.

In closing this observation, I will tell you a quote from a gentleman named Lewis Carroll: IMAGINATION IS THE ONLY WEAPON IN THE WAR AGAINST REALITY. Good luck. Here is a tidbit: ALTRUISM

OBSERVATION TWO

No need for perfection anymore, glitches don't matter

During the corona pandemic I observed something that also made me really change how I will do many things in the future. It is something I touched upon in my first narrative Live Digital or Be Irrelevant. The subject was failure, now I understand what I said because of experience and observation.

A theory I started with was that software is the underbelly of our present future economy but I didn't know why. As I continually observe and deliberate, I came across something called C.I. In English this means CONTINUOUS INTEGRATION. The term is based on the issue that it is impossible to release stable code without a sustainable testing process in place. It is a software development practice that allows individuals to commit changes into a central repository everyday which became mainstream in the 1990's. Once I saw this, I realized this means nothing is ever truly complete. IT IS JUST ONE "BIG SOFTWARE UPDATE". I applied this to the economy and my mind was blown away.

As we have gone through the corona pandemic the Zoom app became a mainstay. It had so many glitches and yet it kept getting downloaded and became indispensable to business and people's personal lives. Even with the glitches people kept on using it. I saw how society had accepted the tech way of doing things, maybe without them realizing it.

For me coming from the independent music business we strived for perfection or to be the best. The goal was to compete with Hollywood and the major labels. However, now that really has been put to rest for me and I will adjust my design accordingly. In the indie music world, we live in the glitch...lol. From what I see now indie (D.I.Y) is cool and credible. It is embedded now in the post corona business model as far as I am concerned. I will of course still strive for perfection but I won't let it stop the whole train from moving.

All of the biggest brands/corporations had to go back to what I call "THE BASICS" during the pandemic. Production went back to guerilla tactics. To sum it up this should motivate all of us to take more chances and do something! I hope you do.

OBSERVATION THREE

Isolation versus Intimacy

I wish to start with the definition of those two words:

Isolation – State of being alone away from others, disconnected, insular.

Intimacy – close, familiarity closeness, private cozy atmosphere, connection.

These two words in my eyes will define our early 2020's as we hurdle to this new post corona economy. People are now isolated with their media/device and air buds. The bulk of people are discovering/entertaining themselves/escaping and killing time in an isolated fashion. However, the key will be the intimacy connection a brand/artist can develop with their audience or individuals.

Big tech has VR/AR ready to take advantage as we move along. The increase of the surveillance/less privacy economy along with contact tracing is here for us now. The isolation experience is regular now as you can watch /listen to something anytime you choose. It gives you the sensation that you are never alone yet you are by yourself. During the early part of the corona pandemic the #ALONETOGETHER was very prevalent. That is a very powerful subliminal message or you can say it is empowering. It all depends on how you are looking are at the world as an individual.

Now let's progress to intimacy. I am saying here that to survive in the post corona time you will have to be PUBLISHED. Your published work online with gatherings being frowned upon by the masses you will have to publish yourself officially to be found. Public/search is the "NEW POWER ECONOMY! If we are isolated then what we publish will be our only way to be heard or found, but more importantly respected. Your reputation will be all you have, so please be very careful with it.

I have established that software is the key underbelly of the economy. I will now say the probability to be drowned out by so much going on will be highly probable. We all will have to circumvent that through intimacy whether that is by knowing the person or how your message can create that intimacy which is the ultimate hook. Since increasingly we will be living through a screen, forming true intimacy will be an ongoing issue to navigate. Your messages/media/content will be your only connection point.

Search/recommendation via the internet will be our survival tools. If the consumer doesn't know you or they do not know your product/service then you are #INTERNETINVISIBLE. That is happening to the masses. The crucial point to this is that this means plenty of people may have never heard of something that is good.

From my observations negative gets noticed more than positive, this is all based on the human condition. You will see I say that here a lot. You will need social chatter or an aggressive ad campaign to get your message through. Recommendations are the way to go. YOU WILL HAVE TO DIVE DEEP INTO THIS SUBJECT! In 2020 you will have to "earn engagement" to have a viable brand or business. No more empty engagement bots, IT HAS TO BE PEOPLE BEHIND IT.

I am going to close on the dangers of isolation. Once you feel alone you can begin to question yourself. That questioning of yourself is what defeats people in their pursuits. The brain never pauses, it can and will play tricks on you. The brain can create a narrative that is baseless and take you through an unnecessary worm hole. Isolation/social distancing has happened in layers. Technology and social media have been distancing people from each other for years! This current corona pandemic just made it so obvious that I hope people can finally see it clearly.

OBSERVATION FOUR

Keep some secrets

For those who don't recognize everything is all in the open and society has been trained to put it all in the open over the past 30 years. I am stating a caveat here: SECRETS WILL BE OF PARAMOUNT IMPORTANCE IN THE POST CORONA WORLD. The human has the capability to keep a secret! It is the almighty human condition that won't allow us to do that. We are designed in theory to-do so. We can hide it in our minds without verbalizing it or writing it down. On the other hand, software will always leave a trail!

As I have stated surveillance trumps privacy going forward in our new world. The human does have issues though, they are ego, pride and greed just to name a few. I feel if the human takes the time to know themselves keeping a secret is very doable. In this post corona world, it will be of paramount importance due to the abundance of life being digital. Data can keep a secret because it is a puzzle of abundance and uses the compelling principle of "hiding in plain sight". That principle is something everyone here needs to deliberate on. Most things you need to better yourself are available to all of us! We just will have to change how we look at the world and what is in it. The key will be to say to yourself EVERYTHING I NEED TO BETTER MYSELF IS IN MYSELF AND IN THE WORLD RIGHT IN FRONT OF ME. This is all a game now and we all have to play in it. You will have to take the time to do so. If you do not take the time no one else will! Each individual must know what to look for, so they can point themselves in the right direction. We must stay away from those worm holes...lol.

The human will have to understand this world is now a "GIANT JIGSAW PUZZLE". You have to be able to put the puzzle together on your own for yourself. The capability to do crossword puzzles or jigsaw puzzles will be very useful in this post corona world. I view the world now as one big jigsaw puzzle the bulk of my day is disseminating all of these pieces that are constantly being made available to us. This generation doesn't do such things and are not being exposed to this, unless the parent brings puzzles to a child it is a skill that is not being nurtured.

In closing, these intangibles will be how we succeed. I will say the human trait of curiosity will be of crucial importance, please dig that out of yourself if you have lost it. BIG TECH DOES NOT TELL

ITS SECRETS! An example of that is the formula that controls their vaunted algorithms that essentially control the world we live in. REMEMBER LEAVE SOMETHING FOR THE IMAGINATION. Good luck!

OBSERVATION FIVE

Strangers through your screen

During this pandemic we all have been sequestered to a screen under the guise of human safety. In the post corona period this will be more prominent even when things get back to quote unquote normal. We have seen meetings and dating be pushed to a screen heavily during this period and socially accepted by most under the guise of human safety. If we view ourselves as pathogens then living our life through a screen will be our life. Meeting strangers through a screen will become the way to live. A screen will become our way of being a human being during this post corona period.

The screen is a filtering system. For those who can remember elementary science you will understand what that means. Let's look at the definition of a filter:

A porous device for removing impurities or solid particles from a liquid or gas passed through it.

We are now living in a filtered society that will be a defining element to our life. Meeting a stranger through a screen will become more human! What I am afraid of we will lose that human element to feel people out. That screen is a safety net. It cuts down on the risk and provides a sense of safety and security. This is all artificial however. I say this because in my past life I spent a dozen years as a night life impresario as a doorman at night club in Manhattan. It was the ultimate moonlighting gig. The reason I bring this this up is because at the end of the day I had to make judgement calls on strangers in less than 30 seconds. Every time you let someone in to the establishment you risk a train wreck taking place. Most people do not understand the severity of that situation. Your business is always at risk. It is an exhaustive process yet now that it is over, I truly understand what took place. I can laugh about some of the episodes now but a lot of people now see it as way too risky to live.

You can't feel fully through a screen. The key is feeling. Feeling is a 6th sense which a screen can't give you because it acts as a filter. In this post corona life to succeed we will need the capability to collaborate and or partner with people/businesses. A device doesn't have feelings. Please remember this. Please do not totally dehumanize yourself.

OBSERVATION SIX

Remote work is the future nobility

During the current pandemic it was quite fascinating to me that governors were telling people to work remote. I was saying to myself who are they talking too? If you are in the people business (human gathering) dealing with a physical footprint (retail stores, restaurants, bars, clubs, gyms, hotels, arenas, stadiums) how can you just work remote? Work remote was code for knowledge worker. It was code for the software economy. It was code for technology especially big tech. It was code given to governors by the think tank/lobbyist who you do not see but are very crucial in making policy that affects your life immensely. THIS WAS VERY PREJUDICIAL TOWARDS CERTAIN PROFESSIONS AND PEOPLE. Throughout my life I have been in both worlds always. I have been in the remote world and I have always worked in the turn key human gathering jobs so I can come and go. With my foundation grounded in the music business you can't have a 9-5. From this pandemic experience I have to divorce myself from the physical world (human gathering) completely and go all the way with the digital component. This was something I already knew but with this pandemic it has sped up my transition to the digital side and cloud-based activities.

The corona pandemic will speed up everyone's transition to remote capabilities, for those of us who are forward thinking. What is so crazy about these times is that trends that I had projected that would take years have now taken weeks and months. In 5 months as I type this August 5th 2020 the economy has adjusted in what would have taken 3-5 years. It would have taken so much more to convince consumers and the global populace to adjust. In my eyes it went from a peaceful transition to a war like environment. In a war like environment you have to speed up production lines and change behavior on the fly. By the time people read this the trends will have moved more violently. We will have to take this under consideration in all of our decision making for the future.

I am stating here a new system of haves and have nots has been formed. Remote workers are at the highest level of society. Think about this you can work or do business anywhere and anytime. This allows opportunity for revenues or client relationships anytime without having to wait. You don't have to go somewhere to make revenue or wages. It is at your own convenience in theory.

Remote work also makes your reach global. This opens up many opportunities to anyone who has the vision to go all in and to take off those mental roadblocks. Remember to attack from an offensive posture not a defensive posture.

Cloud computing had a major test during the pandemic. The gig economy in my eyes was exposed during this time. A GIG IS NOT A JOB. We in the music business are always gigging. It is very cool when it works, but an unbelievable struggle when it doesn't or when there are hiccups. I myself have had 5 years of hiccups.... lol. I like to say, I am living on the banana peel of life. I hope people can see this now and respond accordingly in their future. Unless you are in the music business why would you wish to live the music business life. The holes in the gig economy will not be fixed. You will have to alter your lifestyle design. We have just witnessed the first test of the digital first business model.

In the music business you go in knowing it is no security, it all depends on your hustle. In the gig app world, the advertisements have not exposed this one bit. I myself have been working remote since the 90's when people would laugh at you or insult you. Working remote is all in my DNA. Working remote use to mean you couldn't afford an office space or you didn't have capital in your business. Now it is not a road block and considered cool and credible. YOU LIVE LONG ENOUGH AND YOU SEE IT ALL.

In closing I will go out on a limb that I hope this will help slow down prejudicial behaviors of all kinds. If an employer or client feels a certain way about certain types of people, they will not have to interact with them in a physical space and social settings. What I have just stated I hope will allow the theory of the best person for the job becomes a real principle and not just a wonderful idea. Geography will not matter! The proper question of does the person fit the job based on the skill set needed is the only thing that should be focused on. I know I went out on a limb here but why not. Let's hope that humans really step up. 7/9/20 11:38am.

OBSERVATION SEVEN

Mobility is nobility

Having the capability to conduct business anywhere will allow a whole new level of nobility to take place in people's lives if they can envision it. It is all up to the individual to take control of their existence. Imagine that you don't have to go somewhere to conduct business. This could allow you to do business or work from the beach, if you can imagine it for yourself just to name a place. I am challenging people to imagine. You can hop on and work or hop off. For me that is the only way to live and work going forward. I also thought of this prior but the tech wasn't available in the past. It is a whole new playbook for me to go apply moving forward. I am very amped up and look forward to this incredible experiment. It is up to me to implement this.

I hope we all take the chance to move up the food chain to nobility. NO LIMITS BUT THE LIMITS YOU PUT ON THINGS IN YOUR LIFE. Here is a quote from the book "Pivot to the Future" by Omar Abbosh, Paul Nunes and Larry Downes: Transforming your old businesses to embrace new technology and create the fuel for growth as oppose to getting rid of them. Now industry evolves at the pace of its fastest changing technology. Once you bring digital to an industry you must evolve at a digital pace. I call it Live Digital or be Irrelevant.

The crux of the cloud/devices/data is for them to enhance your lifestyle. It challenges each individual to constantly evolve and adapt continuously. No more getting comfortable. Unless you are going to check out from all of this you will have to constantly evolve and adapt. Stop and deliberate on what I just said here. What I am essentially saying here the old easy roads are done. It will be a new easy road of constant adapting. The industrial age is being put out to pasture. If you don't understand what I saying here you will have to take a deep dive into what the industrial age really was. That is something you will have to do on your own time. I feel you should if you have not in the past.

In this post corona economy, your saving grace will be to allow yourself to do what is necessary to go to this present future nobility. Prior to the corona pandemic I was on the fast track to move to south east Asia for a year but that is on hold now. That is my remote/mobility is nobility. The last time I did this I moved to London to launch my record label Prohibition Entertainment just when Napster was finding its conversation with the music industry. I hope to still do this but with the corona pandemic gobbling up the world, I am monitoring the situation closely. I have redesigned my plans and will use my total tool shed to make this happen.

In closing, get behind mobility is nobility. On a side note I was supposed to finish this narrative on the other side of the world but you have to adapt. I have a 3rd narrative I will conceive where ever I end up. Stay tuned.

OBSERVATION EIGHT

Being an actor versus a reactor

Here are the most compelling theorems I will share in my eyes, that will be defining your upward or down ward trajectory in the future. Here are two quotes that we will have to digest over and over. We must constantly refer to them daily in our future:

1. The biggest advantage you have in this business is your own voice. Your own way of looking at things, your own way of thinking about things. That is where your power lies. - DAN WEIDEN THE AUTHOR OF JUST DO IT BY NIKE
2. If you see it when no one else see's it then you got to do it if you believe! Based on Steve Job's why 1984 won't be like 1984 Super Bowl Commercial.

Here is the critical part of it all... both of these campaigns were questioned by the internal teams. We like to think that everyone knew what they were doing and it was all pre-determined. We like to think that it was all figured out. However, it wasn't. I hope this information makes you meditate on things. Both individuals held their ground and said this is it. It worked those times but how many times it didn't? That doesn't matter, you need a magical moment once that stands the test of time and you will be good.

Analysis: I AM SAYING HERE THAT THIS WILL BE THE AGE OF YOU HAVING YOUR OWN VOICE! YOU WILL HAVE TO BE AN ACTOR NOT A REACTOR. LET'S LOOK AT DEFINITIONS:

Actor – A participant in an action or process.

Reactor – Catalyst. One that reacts.

In this post corona economy, you must be an actor. To quote my 7th grade music teacher Mr. Habash "this is an open and shut case". You must be leading not following. Those are the people who will win. You have to be able to draw interest. YOU MUST GET IN FRONT OF SOMETHING TO PUT IT BLUNTLY. Whatever it is you have to be the face or the voice of it. You have to start the fire and have ownership of it. You must develop what I am labelling #BIGTRUST. You have heard of big tech, big oil and big pharma, going forward businesses/brands but especially personal brands must have big trust. This will be your meal ticket in this present future. You have to be a player now. I am use to operating from behind the scenes but my "long moonlight" as part of my night life experiment, I developed that "BIG TRUST" which lead to many things called success. This led to the Sullivan Room winning the "Night Stalker Award " against clubs worldwide. I proud to say I was an important cog in that operation. That was however, offline. I will be transferring that to my online life that I am jump starting now. I will not call my process branding; I am stating here that word has been abused like most things in this era we now live in. I am calling it #bigtrust, you read it here first.

If people trust you in the post corona present future, they will be more liable to collab with you or engage with what you have published. This big trust will make sharing easier! Tik Tok is the epitome of this phenomenal process. That big trust will in theory bring big revenue to what you are doing because of the massive engagement.

You will have to draw a line in the sand in this present future. There will be no shortcuts. You can't hide behind someone or something else and expect to have success. Those looking for shortcuts, what I call the "diet pill syndrome" this is not for you.

We all have to figure out how we will be that actor, to not be in the sea of reactors. In this environment you will have to keep learning at an exponential rate. It is not about working hard anymore, that is the industrial revolution "tricknology" that was placed on the masses 150 years ago. To now thrive and survive we have to constantly learn, but here is the crucial difference from the industrial age you will have to unlearn very frequently. I brought this up in my first narrative the idea of unlearning. #LEARNHARDNOTWORKHARD is our secret sauce. Your message will get you the volunteers not paid staff that is necessary in this time. You will have to inspire people. Please stop here and deliberate before going on to the next observation. Good luck

OBSERVATION NINE

From Haves & Have Nots to now Knows & Know Nots

In the post corona economy, there will be a new dual level of wealthy in our society. We will of course still have the old fashion #HAVESANDHAVENOTS, but I am announcing a new class of people #THEKNOWSANDKNOWNOTS. The "HAVES AND KNOWS" are separate, but can be also be one of the same. In this information/data/algorithm driven society it will be one thing to be a "Have Not" but now to be a "Know Not" will be a double whammy placed on people which will be very punitive. THOSE WHO ARE IN THE KNOW CLASS WILL BE ABLE TO GRADUATE TO THE HAVE CLASS I FEEL, BUT IF YOU ARE A KNOW NOT THEN YOU WILL HAVE THE DOUBLE WHAMMY ON YOU. Absolutely no politician will be telling the voters or the masses of people this very pertinent fact of life. This observation is worth the price of the book!

In the past you had to navigate the physical or analogue world, now you have to navigate the digital world even if you don't want to because it has such a dynamic effect on your life that the politicians will not tell the people. WE ARE LIVING IN TWO WORLDS NOW! You have two very distinct worlds to navigate with the same 24 hours. We are constantly going in two worlds now.

What I am discussing here in this narrative is to become more of a "Know Person" and escape #knownotism. I do know now to become a HAVE you will have to be a "KNOW". YOU CAN BE A "HAVE NOT" AND BE A "KNOW" AND STILL BECOME A "HAVE"! A "Know Not" will have no chance to be a ""HAVE"" unless they are reading what I am writing here and take a huge interest in the digital economy not wasting every passing day, that will only elongate the process to have any chance of becoming a "HAVE". The state lottery will be the only way for people to move up the social ladder. Marrying upward to get to the "HAVE" part of society has been altered in my eyes due to the dating app culture. If we take a look at the statistical odds of hitting the lottery then you know why the government has essentially barged in on organized crime's racket of cash flow. Marrying upwardly is now even not for Hollywood movies. Due to the way society is arranged now with the digitization of dating with the apps with their preferences and interest marrying upward has taking a hit, the dream is mostly over. The "KNOWS" know what may have made you successful in the 20th century can be shackles in the

21th century economy. The term disruption comes to mind. The "KNOWS" know the battle is to stay relevant because quote un quote facts keep changing abruptly. The economy is now set up to continually transform! The" KNOWS" know most of us look back instead of looking ahead. The masses live in the memories i.e. back in the day syndrome. Nostalgia is always referenced by the masses. When the world changes around us we tend to stop looking to learn because people get flabbergasted or fearful. I look at it as they run out of positive fuel and their tanks filled with negative fuel. Instead of looking at our own internal self, we will blame other things.

The "KNOWS" know that with this present future you must have the ability to have a vision of your own of the future and have the imagination that will allow you to escape the constraints of the past to enter fresh territory that opens up possibilities of opportunities. They know the future isn't fixed. The future to the "KNOWS" is permeable and you have the ability to reconstruct your personal narratives always. The "KNOWS" know it is your network, your surroundings and where you place yourself to spend your time will be what is most critical to change your business or your life. The "KNOWS" know we are living on a constant threshold that is exciting yet full of risk. Please remember continuous integration…that is our future. In the industrial age stability was prized. That is gone now. I will suggest to navigate your way to the "KNOW" class of people for a dynamic future.

OBSERVATION TEN

Big picturism will be needed

- You can't control events but you do control your response to events. - Stoic philosophy from 2000 years ago
- Public relations as far as I am concern has gone through a slow death. It is now based on the comment section via social media

These two premises will be so crucial for a person or business. How we respond to events will be a pertinent part of our future because the tools are always there for us. Use them correctly and productively.

The goal of the digital universe is to micro target not macro target. You must really deliberate on this point as it will be very crucial to your decision making, that will define your growth.

In this post corona time period, we always will have forks in the road. We now have a spellbinding amount of decisions daily to be made due to the prolific amount of information in the market place.

Let's look at the definitions of micro and macro -

Micro – Extremely small. Involving a nanoscopic variation.

Macro – Large scale.

The reason I am discussing this is because even though we will be spending most of our time in the digital (micro) world, more and more we must maintain big picture thinking in all we do. In my eyes we have been led away from macro thinking. We have been led away from critical thinking because in the world of "GOOGLE IT" most things can be found in a quick efficient fashion. Let's look at the definition of efficient -

A system or machine achieving maximum productivity with minimum wasted effort or expense. Humans are not efficient because they are complex creative creatures, yet everywhere I look we are told to be more efficient. Computers are efficient but humans are not.

Post corona remote entertainment will stay with us. I feel this major behavioral shift will remain in place. People have been embedded at home for 5 months now as of August 2020 as I complete this manuscript. This process has been imprinted into people now.... the human is a pathogen and that you should be leery of strangers especially. Here are trends that I feel will be crucial:

- The attention wars will grow immensely as everyone is fighting for each other's time.
- Ownership of media I.P will have heightened importance. WHOEVER MOVES THE NEEDLE WILL BE THE WINNER AND WILL ACQUIRE A GROWING BUSINESS AND BIG TRUST. WE must figure out how to be consistent on that.
- QUALITY WILL DEFEAT QUANTITY. QUALITY FOR AWHILE LOST ITS WAY BUT WILL BE BACK STRONGLY.
- You will have to share a piece of yourself in the future.

In closing, we are in a unique time, I feel there is opportunity to invent but more importantly reinvent your own future, if you are willing to see it. EMBRACE THAT THOUGHT.

OBSERVATION ELEVEN

Algorithms are making all the decisions (Part 2)

Let's start with the definition in this oh so important word which is controlling so much of our lives. Algorithm: Is a procedure or formula for solving a problem based on conducting a sequence of specified actions. A computer program can be viewed as an elaborate algorithm. In mathematics and computer science an algorithm usually means a small procedure that solves a recurrent problem.

Every day we have to deal with an algorithm in our daily lives. Even if you just go on Facebook to talk to your extended family or friends every so often you are interacting with an algorithm. If you are on Instagram cruising around looking at photos or posting your own photos you are interfacing with an algorithm. If you are watching videos on You Tube you are engaging with an algorithm. The same for Twitter, Spotify and Amazon.

Consider this algorithm similar to the Wizard of Oz behind the curtain. For those who may miss the reference please watch the movie when you get a spare 2 hours. The algorithm is making decisions constantly that control what you see and hear. I will put it bluntly here, the technology is hacking human feelings, attitudes, beliefs and behaviors. The algorithm keeps people engaged with products /services/ media etc. I am trying here in a short space to get individuals to understand what is really happening to us on a daily basis. To cut to the chase, I need everyone here to visualize a gigantic computer pointed at your brain every single day! STOP HERE AND MEDITATE ON THAT FOR FEW MOMENTS. The post corona economy is based on that premise. During this corona pandemic an article in techcrunch.com said: Facebook and telephone companies building a huge subsea cable for Africa and the middle east. Facebook, China mobile international, MTN global connect, Orange and Vodafone are collaborating on this cable. I pose the question here so you can ask yourself why are they spending a huge amount of money to reach all of these impoverish people? The project is called 2 Africa www.2africacable.com. I am here to get people to see the future before it happens. Hopefully, you can place yourself in position to prosper on these trends. The algorithm is deeply involved with this. These companies understand our future. They are placing big bets! You must bet on yourself! I WILL POSE THE QUESTION HERE:

WHAT BIG BET WILL YOU PLACE ON YOURSELF? Those cables I discussed above will allow the algorithm of Facebook to be fed much more!

Where do you fit in all of this? These cables are needed to allow the data factory to continue to grow. These companies need to connect the people in those areas to the internet to feed that algorithm. Once the cable is laid that device (smart phone) is weaponized. THOSE CABLES WILL ALLOW POTENTIALLY ALL OF THOSE PEOPLE TO BE ADDED TO THE GLOBAL DATA FACTORY! At the end of the day who is the product? We are the product... the humans all over the planet. We are here to feed that algorithm. I suggest you dig real deep into this to understand what this means for humanity on the planet moving forward. Please stop and think!!

In closing, I will discuss dating briefly and how it relates to algorithms. I am stating here that dating apps are putting people in "preference hell". We like to think we know what we really want, I feel love has a mind of its own I still believe. The dating apps are making dating a robotic process and not a human one. It is micro not macro. I see love as those intangibles, not a check list of preferences. I know times have changed but have they really? Please understand you can't date an algorithm, only a person.

OBSERVATION TWELVE

Going viral is a short-term goal post

The reason why I say this is because going viral will reach many, but the key for you to win will be how many people engage with you and your media/service/content. LET ME REPEAT, WHO INTERACTS WITH YOU AND COMMENTS. Remember I discussed time, and attention remember, what did I say is the most precious and equalizing resource.... TIME. Going viral is the beginning not the end game. In most online marketing everyone is pushing going viral but it is not explained what to do prior and after. What also isn't said is that trends (going viral) come and go. The social media algorithms are set up to spew out trends to bring attention to whatever it is. Going viral is hitting the internet lottery! Winning the "HUNGER GAMES". You have to have the foundation in place to take advantage of that fleeting notoriety. There are no guarantees in this global hunger games. People are infatuated with going viral because it is tossed about now every day. Going viral is luck as well as a process. It takes a foundation and a developed skill set to do, which comes with studying the internet dynamic and how it truly works.

The thing about the internet is that you have to go beyond looking at something, you have to begin to see it. You will have to take the time to understand each platform and what it does. For example, Instagram is different than Twitter. You Tube is different than Tik Tok. You must take the time to have a broad understanding of these platforms and how they are utilized in the going viral process.

A lot of going viral is a robotic automation. You must dig into that deeper on your own. Please remember getting in front of people is not the issue anymore. It is less about selling online, it is about building a narrative! You must understand that. IT IS NOT ABOUT HITTING THE LOTTERY WHICH IS USUALLY A ONE TIME EVENT. YOU HAVE TO BUILD A CREDIBLE NARRATIVE THAT PEOPLE WILL CARE ABOUT IN THE POST CORONA WORLD! Something that people are searching for! Going viral is a one and done!

The crux will be search! Search is the most powerful and dynamic thing around. The bedrock of Google is its search engine. Please understand and dig deeper into that. You will have to understand and keep up with your platform's priorities to increase your chance of getting the most from these platforms.

You must ask yourself how will your campaign/product improve people's lives? WHY SHOULD THEY PAY ATTENTION TO WHAT YOU ARE OFFERING?

In closing, the key to induce organic virality I feel is to keep the story compact so people hopefully seeing it will spark a new story about themselves. THAT IS WHY A CONTEST WORKS SO WELL. Here is crucial hack: Tell the story from the audience's agenda if you can. It is these small granular details that online will make a difference. YOU WILL NEED DEPTH NOT JUST NUMBERS. Please focus on depth and detail going forward.

OBSERVATION THIRTEEN

Media is lumped together now. Culture is what is separate now.

Steve Jobs via iTunes started the disintermediation of media. It is all lumped together. Fast forward to 2020, it is all just one big melting pot. Books, Music, Film, TV, Documentaries, podcasts etc. It is all competing for consumers limited time! It is still only 24 hours in a day. This is why I said in my case it is no more music industry. It is all media and time consumption.

Culture is the now the key to it all. What culture are you a part of? What culture are you speaking to? Who are you speaking to? Culture is what separates us and bring us together at the same time. I will mostly discuss how it brings us together and how media is fuel. Let's look at the definition of culture:

The customs, arts, social institutions and achievements of a particular nation, people or other social group. It derives from the Latin word colere which means tend to the earth and grow or cultivation and nurture.

Culture is what interest people! Culture is what people do.... How they live. Why they live. Their interest and most important how they exist. What feeds them mentally and spiritually. With the internet being "supreme maggot overlord" there is culture for every little niche. THE INTERNET HAS CREATED THOUSANDS OF NICHE CULTURES. You have to really know what, how and why you will fit into a culture. Prior to something going mainstream (mass market or viral) it has to start somewhere in culture. Whatever you propose has to get in where it can fit in. YOU MUST ASK YOURSELF WHERE DO I FIT IN BEST? You may fit in multiple places but what place on the granular level do you fit in best to launch what you are proposing? Moving culture when there is so much going on is a great task. In this age of social media everyone technically has a voice in culture. Everyone can be an organizer, broadcaster, blogger and communicator.

In the old times prior to the 2000's information spreading was an expensive proposition. Culture was fueled from the USA'S and European narrative. In this time of the cheap smart phone being the main device and social media being so prominent new rules of engagement have impacted culture! Here is a powerful statement that hopefully simplifies even more what I am conveying here:

YOU DO NOT HAVE TO CHANGE THE WORLD YOU JUST NEED TO CHANGE SOMEONE'S WORLD.

That is what the goal is for me now. Even though we live in an exponential world with all of the technology, it can still be used incrementally to impact culture. YOU CAN GO GRANULAR! There are many ways to use exponential technology to impact culture. What I am truly trying to do here is show you that there are no resolute rules. There are principles and processes but it is up to the individual how they choose to use the technology.

IN CLOSING, CULTURE HAS NO GEOGRAPHICAL CONSTRAINTS. YOU CAN IMPACT FROM ANYWHERE. Take all of this in. Please deliberate on this. Use these platforms to their fullest capabilities. Scan the cultural landscape on a daily basis...AN OPPORTUNITY AWAITS.

OBSERVATION FOURTEEN

How do you see the world?

In my eyes each individual through their own experiences are unique granularly to themselves. We have to spend the time questioning ourselves on how that difference can be marketed. This means we have to spend time inside ourselves to find that. In my first narrative I discussed the U in unique. If you can find that intangible that only you have and then use it productively, you have a better chance of winning. It will allow you to differentiate yourself. Most of us want what we can't have which is part of what is called the HUMAN CONDITION. Only you have walked in your shoes because no one else can. Dig deep into that statement please. Your lens to the world is different than mine. We have to find our own answers we usually do not take the time to investigate to find them.

Search for those "intangible experiences" that most won't have. I think I found some for myself and are using them. Please take the time to find yours asap and use them to craft a story that can impact a part of culture that you can connect to. All we are doing is bringing another point of view to this global table of contents. The best thing we all can do is bring one that is unique and may stand out.

Use the technology we have access to but do not glorify the technology. GLORIFY YOUR UNIQUE SELF OR IDEA....Your unique message. Here is a caveat – The human condition will reject new things.... unique things... unproven things. Be ready to defend your U in unique. Good luck the next observation preps you.

OBSERVATION FIFTEEN

From dead ends to What ifs!

What I have learned is to take a shortage of capital and the shortage of personnel off the table coming from the independent music world. Those two things are always limited assets. However, for me over the last three years I decided to take those elements off of the table and say what if.... What if I really embrace digital not just use a computer but explore what digital means? How to not reject digital possibilities but openly say to myself what if.... Now what if is one of the first things I say. I live the perilous art of the possible". Delving into this what if world which usually has no market or a limited precedent and appears so distant, most people will run away from your what if. YOU HAVE TO INCUBATE YOUR PROPOSAL with yourself first.

In this what if world you will have to construct and reconstruct. You are looking for the smallest thread of proof of concept or idea. When you are pitching you start off by saying imagine this.... Even the most obstinate type of individual does have some imagination left in them. Explain diligently what happens without the idea or concept. Do not use facts or evidence like a lawyer but use the five senses especially sight and sound. Those things are beneficial to getting your message through.

Here is perspective from Sir Arthur Clarke the inventor of Geo stationary communication satellites and a major author of a dozen sci books, he called it the evolution of ideas:

a. Crazy – It will never work, in this post corona world of technological culture and information creative ideas/concepts are the ultimate resource.
b. Oh, it might work but not worth the effort.
c. I told you it was a great idea.

In this future time, we have to continuously go off the reservation. You will have to leave the cocoon of safety. Most importantly as I realized when I conceived my first narrative there is no failure, it is all a learning experience. FAILURE IS THE MOST CRITICAL COMPONENT FOR BREAK

THROUGHS. That attitude is pivotal for success and growth. I have grown to be more concerned of losing out on potential AHA MOMENTS. The more you can do it the easier it gets.

A caveat is that you will probably have to face down any negative bias thrown your way. This is when you know that you have graduated to the next level when you continue your trail. To get the naysayers on board will be tough. The goal is getting someone who can bring credibility to the concept of what you are proposing on to the team to go from possibility to probability. Imagination will be your greatest weapon in this post corona economy. Only hungry minds will succeed here! That is what we possess as individuals.

Here is a quote from Alvin Toffler:

The key in the 21st century economy will not be those who can read and write but those who can learn, unlearn and relearn.

To me imagination or Imagineering is unlearning because you are going someplace very unfamiliar. Good luck with this process that I am using myself.

OBSERVATION SIXTEEN

Data and The Death Of Random

Internet products/services are modelled to cut down the level of risk and increase automation. The products and services attempt to take out the random element in our lives. They attempt to be predictive based on your past behavior. They use recommendations that attempt to take out the surprise. Make the unknown known. The whole purpose of this push to a data driven society is to take out the randomness of life. Too me randomness has been depicted as a fearful thing if you are listening and watching how society is moving now.

I will say here depending on data will have you looking backwards! A lot of folks haven't really thought about that statement. Data has already happened! It appears neat and orderly. It is a false security blanket in my eyes. It makes you feel secure in your actions. This data dependence gives us the appearance of making smart and intelligent decisions. The key message I want you to take in is that data has you looking backwards. It has told you what has happened but not necessarily what will happen. I know what I am saying is going against the grain of what is put forth on a daily basis by experts and data scientists etc., but I am standing by it. The data is attempting to impersonate a crystal ball. Data can show you a trail of things but it can't show you the future and that is what the masses are being led to believe that it can do... fortune telling. It cannot do the thinking for you.

What people have to remember is that this data is generated by human actions. As I said earlier humans are complex creatures that are not fully understood. Humans will do things that are a mystery and we have questions. Humans will do random things that can only make sense to themselves in the moment. The data can help but it is not exact. You still have to question the data. I feel that people have forgotten to question it.

I recall in high school at good old Brooklyn Tech in my electrical engineering class that one of the things the teacher said was G.I.G.O = Garbage in Garbage Out. I do not here that anymore when I read and absorb technology-based information. The appearance is given that the computer is right and the human is wrong. G.I.G.O is still very real to me. In this world of data that we live in, if you put "flawed data" into a computer what do you think will take place? The response or report will be flawed.

GARBAGE IN GARBAGE OUT. For people to survive in this post corona time it will be critical for anyone to still be able to think for themselves. The data is to assist you but not to give you the answer. The data is just a tool just like a device, it is not to be worshipped or fawned over.

The human brain is the true computer of the world and it is being used less and less. The human brain is a muscle that also needs to work out and receive maintenance. Do not give up the idea of randomness. Do not be afraid of it and please do not forget that it exists. I still embrace and look forward to randomness. It is exciting but mostly it will keep you ahead of the game. THE BUSINESSES I AM IN I THRIVE FOR THE YOU NEVER KNOW. Data can't give you that randomness which is your secret sauce.

OBSERVATION SEVENTEEN

The wild west of falsehood is our new media world

This for me is my most favorite observation and it ties into G.I.G.O in my last observation. Here is a powerful quote, I do not recall where I got it from:

THE TRUTH IS LEARNED.... NEVER TOLD.

Please stop and meditate on that quote because it will be crucial to your future.

I am stating here we live in a revolving state of subterfuge and obfuscation in the 21st century economy. Let's look at the definitions of both quickly:

Subterfuge – deceit used to achieve one's goal.

Obfuscation – render obscure, unclear, or unintelligible, bewilder someone.

These two words will be needed to navigate the 21st century. Here is a quick review. Via social media anyone has a voice. Anyone can place something online. The question is will it be picked up or just lost in the black whole of the internet. What is placed online does not have to be fact checked. Fact checking is a principle in journalism, something that has seen a steady decline in the digital era. In fact, journalism is not being done in the majority of the world now. Journalism is a profession and is work! A lot of the things that are now shown to people are at their best op-eds or whimsical work. Getting to a fact based or truthful angle is not the way things work in this new media landscape. WE LIVE NOW IN AN ENVIRONMENT OF SHIFTING AGENDAS. You need to stop and deliberate on that statement.

We are now conditioned to be a skeptic in the "false news" era that we live in. News is fact checked and is based on integrity. False news is based on agendas. YOU MUST STOP AND MEDITATE ON THAT. Due to the fact that most people are now trained that it if it is on their device it must be credible. I won't say truthful but credible. Getting to the truth will be much harder if not impossible now in this time we live in. Now let's please go back to obfuscation and the truth is learned for a moment, credible is the key now as you move forward in your new digital lifestyle because credible people or institutions have SOMETHING TO LOSE. On the internet your credibility will be your currency. Credible organizations do not wish to lose that. This is why the concept of character assassination will be used by individuals with agendas. Others who have nothing to lose are the majority online. Social media is based on opinions, agendas and whatever sounds good. Facts also, but it all depends who is using it.

Caveat emptor is to be used on the internet always. In this internet age a rumor that has zero basis yet sounds plausible and interesting enough can spread around the world in hours and then just dissipate. However, the damage it can cause maybe irreversible. Here is a wonderful quote from Sir Winston Churchill:

A lie gets half way around the world before the truth has a chance to gets its pants on.

This is why I call it the wild west of falsehood. WE NOW LIVE IN THE WORLD OF "PLAUSIBLE INFORMATION". It sounds legit but if you start questioning you will see the holes. Questioning takes the most precious resource we have which is time. In this 24/7 scrolling down on your phone society, we now live in a gray world not a black and white one.

As we move along, you will have to become a journalist and take the time to fact check, research something which is a very invasive procedure. You may have to check those footnotes to be sure. You will have to most definitely check who is bankrolling an organization or platform during this time to be as through as possible. We are always walking into a minefield of agendas now impersonating credible news. In America we live in the age of polarization within the media space. It is all about agendas. We move further and further away from objectivity and historical record. If something is coming from what is called "the left", the people on the quote unquote right do not believe the narrative and vice versa. IT CAN BE SHAMED, SLAMMED AND FINALLY CALLED PARTISAN EVEN IF IT IS THE QUOTE UN QUOTE TRUTH.

Social media has taken us back to junior high school on a daily basis I feel. Think about it, we have to "like something" or give it a thumbs up or down. Just because we may not like something doesn't make it not truthful or full of facts. This goes back to eating your vegetables, just because you don't like it doesn't make it not good for you.

The news is now curated based on if we like something! The algorithms remember what you looked at in the past and gives you what you seem to want, not what you may need to be aware of in the moment. As I said, humans are complexed evolving creatures. This is why I said we live now in a world of questions as much as I am still looking for some answers. I HAVE TO KEEP QUESTIONING TO STAY RELEVANT.

I hope the puzzle is coming together for you here. THE METHOD TO THE MADNESS. Here is a quote from the chief information officer of M&T Bank in May 2020:

To win in a world that is becoming more networked you will need to be a network yourself.

If you don't pull together as a community you lose. PLEASE LOOK AT YOUR NETWORK! STOP AND LOOK AT YOUR NETWORK NOW! We are living in a world of "attention wars". How do you get people's attention? From my assessment you get it with "negative fuel" much faster than with "positive fuel". Any two-bit psychologist knows that! This is why the media (news) is mostly on a negative posture not a positive one. You must understand the news has to get ratings, it is a business based on profit and loss. It is not here to serve people.

You must remember everyone is being heard now. In the past that wasn't possible. I feel with this power comes a responsibility. We must understand what we say, how we say it can be impactful. People don't understand "contextual' 'thought", but more importantly we don't have the time to understand. If you have no idea what that is, you can see how quote unquote false news can spread like wildfire. Please stop, think and meditate on what I just said.

We have agendas being played out every day, make no mistake about that! In the past the subjects of ethics, morals and integrity were placed in schools or at least in homes. These subjects were discussed as you moved along to adulthood. In this 21st century economy those things have become disposable. It is up to the individuals/businesses for these crucial threads to be part of your internal constitution. The human element is the bedrock of all of this digital economy, please do not forget this when you are holding your device in your hands. It can do positive things or negative things, please be very careful with it. I SEE A MORAL AND ETHICAL SCARCITY UPON US AS WE MOVE DEEPER INTO THE 2020'S.

Think about this for a moment please, we went from the Pony Express being a disruptive force in the 1860's, to a Twitter account and smart phone in the 2010's which allows you now to communicate freely around the globe in seconds. Add in a webcam and now you have the capability to go live and "narrowcast" your message in a very cost-effective fashion. The only thing that is not free is the time! I hope you see I keep going back to that 4-letter word. I will define broadcast and narrowcast:

Narrowcast – transmit a tv program by cable or otherwise disseminate information, to a comparatively small audience defined by special interest or geographical location.

Broadcast – scatter or sow over a broad area to make it widely known.

I will argue here now we live in the age of narrowcasting. Please understand that going forward. You also do not need big cameras or a TV station or radio station to get your message out. All of those things were expensive in the past which allowed a limited amount of people to dominate the narrative. Smart phones being so cheap the rules of engagement have forever changed. An example of this, Hollywood produces approximately 500 films a year up to 2019, at 2 hours per movie this about 1000 hours. You Tube producers upload 48 hours' worth of video a minute. The silent majority now has a large yet miniscule voice. In my main business as of summer 2020 60,000 songs a day allegedly are being released, for me that just sounds insane.

As you can see, I have spent the most time on this area because it is actually the most crucial in what we do with our most precious commodity…. time. Also, of great importance, is the idea we never know how far our message can go. My point with this narrative is to point people in the right direction. In this era, we are drowning in false knowledge (information), everywhere you can see pundits, gurus and consultants (I do not claim to be any of those titles) who are all spouting theories? They appear to know so much, yet have to deliver so little. IT IS OPINION AND SPIN, PROMISE WITHOUT PERFORMANCE and ACCOUNTS WITHOUT ACCOUNTABILITY. I have used everything written here to reinvent my lifestyle and relaunch my business. For me this is what I do and I understand the importance of everything that was said here.

Due to all of the elements happening in our society what I am calling the "lazy brain society" is prevalent. Deception is being represented always from all imaginable angles. This is all burying original thought/critical thinking/ due to all of the noise and very organized confusion. A thoughtful point of view is what is scarce now. THAT IS THE SECRET SAUCE. Remember to ask:

a. You must ask yourself, who am I speaking to.
b. How do they want to be spoken to?
c. Where do we speak with them?

These falsehoods are a form of censorship because they disconnect people from reality causing people to believe and do things way off the reservation. They get people going down the wrong lane which will end up poorly for people. Things go left quickly on people because their actions diverge from the construct of reality. With the extreme acceleration of information to survive and be productive you must be able to tell the difference between real and fake. That is the most important thing we can do in this time period.

During the corona pandemic three new states were ratified in the USA. The states of Hysteria, Paranoia and Panic. Please do not move to any of those new states. These places keep you blind to what is really going on around you. GOOD LUCK NAVIGATING THIS EVERYDAY WILD WEST OF FALSEHOOD.

OBSERVATION EIGHTEEN

Digital content pollution

I was deliberating on some notes and the idea of pollution kept coming across my mind. Then I decided to apply it to the digital space and boy it really it hit the spot. Let's look at the various definitions:

Pollution is something introduced into the environment that is dirty, unclean or has a harmful effect. It is the introduction of contaminants into a natural environment that causes adverse change. It has a great effect on the environment.

Now let's apply this to our digital world we live in and our future. It is very scary to me! Most people who are and will be damaged by all of this digital pollution are uneducated, the impoverish and the under educated which is now a very fluid category. How about the ignorant. Remember the" KNOW NOTS" I mentioned earlier.

Digital pollution is truly an everyday tsunami. It is a tidal wave of digital pollution being delivered every day and we all add to it because we have an opinion. The digital pollution can only increase with the billions scheduled to join us online in the coming years. In this narrative I have already discussed many things that are on the periphery of this subject that many do not think about. The best solution is for individuals to find the time to keep learning so they can be as unaffected as possible from all of this digital pollution that comes through our phones every single day. Our brains and mental psyche do get affected by this pollution immensely and this must be accounted for in our daily lives.

Education I feel is very needed to assist in this growing fight against "digital pollution". I see immense pollution every day. It can be labelled fake news but for the most part it is called information or content. I want to say here I am not for censorship either. However, the free flow of information in theory allows everyone a chance to get a message out, we truly have freedom of speech and a lot of disagreement comes with that. As I finalize this manuscript (August 9th-11th) there is a lot of censorship taking place on the big social platforms such as Facebook, Twitter and You Tube which is something that appears now to be picking up steam. I feel in order for the premise of freedom speech to matter the individual before they press send needs to reflect on what they are "gifting" the world. The individual must say is this worthwhile! How will this be impactful and what way will this be helpful. I know this is delusional...lol, but I have to maintain a hopeful slant toward the human condition.

The same way that air pollution, noise pollution and water pollution is of critical importance, I feel the idea of #digital pollution will be of growing importance. DIGITAL POLLUTION DAMAGES THE MIND/PSYCHE/SOUL OF THE INDIVIDUAL AND CAUSES MASSIVE CONFUSION TO THE MASSES WHO UNAWARE OF IT'S CONSEQUENCES. I am just trying to open up the discussion here.

I am going to close using a quote from one of the founding fathers who had a very large impact on the constitution James Madison:

KNOWLEDGE WILL FOREVER GOVERN IGNORANCE AND THE PEOPLE WHO MEAN TO BE THEIR OWN GOVERNORS MUST ARM THEMSELVES WITH THE POWER WHICH KNOWLEDGE GIVES. Thank you for allowing me to bring this subject to the light. 6/11/20 2:52pm

OBSERVATION NINETEEN

Redefinition of the live event

In the post corona economy, the device is now an arena, stadium, night club or performance space. Via your phone/tablet you can watch a concert with your cocktail in the privacy of your own living room. It will be through a screen not necessarily a place! I AM DISCUSSING FROM A MUSIC BUSINESS PERSPECTIVE, BUT SINCE I FEEL THAT EVERY SINGLE PERSON OR BUSINESS IS IN THE MUSIC BUSINESS NOW, IT ALL CONNECTS NOW TO OTHER BUSINESSES OR LIFESTYLES.

In China music and social are linked at the hip, due to the fact they do not have all of the "heritage media" that we have here in the west. China didn't have commercial radio, college radio, community radio, public radio, mix shows, club DJ's etc. Their music industry is connected through social and gaming. Those trends are starting to explode here now in 2020. The music industry there is not an incubated business like in the west. They possess a different set of rules. The live music side of the business is part of the kinetic energy and not seen as separate.

The reason I digress to this subject is because social media is all about the device. The China music business was totally designed simpatico with the devices and the social/sharing element baked into the design. Live is not a separate business like how it is in the west. However, the west is now changing. I am looking to Asia to see what live will be like. I will say they are ahead of us but the corona virus has forced us to move ahead much quicker. Prior to the corona pandemic I was monitoring these trends closely and is why I said Corona has sped up these trends up immensely. We add in the 5G broadband which China/Singapore are moving faster than we are and you can begin to see what will happen next. You should go on Google and do a deep dive into this because the speed of this is going to be compelling.

I am going to focus on the macro trend here to give you some insight yet it is just the tip of the iceberg. Spaces will increasingly become virtual and wired. The corona will only speed this up! Paywalls will be added so people can get the experience via there oculus or device. Remember with the human being viewed as a pathogen this trend in my eyes will have to fulfill itself. The stay at home quarantine people are now "preconditioned" for this. It is now baked in our cultural DNA. Before the pandemic

Coachella via You Tube's annual Coachella live stream was growing nicely incrementally but now with the pandemic this will grow exponentially. The broadcast of this is called "COUCHELLA".

Forward thinking clubs are wiring their venues. I read an article on www.toronto.com that discussed a company called CYA that will wire an entire venue, from the stage, to the dressing rooms, for high quality live streaming enhanced experiences. Other clubs /venues will have to do this also. I have seen that alcohol and music are not enough anymore. I was part of a new club opening in 2018 in the meat packing district in New York City and I saw a huge difference from 2013 when the Sullivan Room venue was closed abruptly. I saw that music and alcohol wasn't enough and this generation demands so much more from a venue experience. Other clubs will have to do this. Venues in Asia will be ahead of us. The massive upfront investment for this will alter the economics of opening a night club venue.

If we tie in 5G and we have a whole exponential experience here. You just have to take the time to connect the dots. All I can say is OMG. Samsung in the summer of 2019 introduced the vertical stage called the KX. I dialed into this this immediately because of music but fast forward post corona and it was genius to do this. I completely understood because my business plan from 2016–2017 was all based on the smart phone and mobile activity. Now in the post corona all I can say is OMG. The premise of the stage design is based on the fact that most people prefer to take photos vertically and see the world from that perspective. With Instagram being so prevalent with over 100 million photos taken daily you can see where this is going, I hope. The KX stage was built vertically not horizontally which is essentially designed for the smart phone. You must incorporate shooting vertically in your business design.

If you look at the post corona economy and the human is being viewed as a pathogen you see where the pieces of the puzzle will come together. What does Samsung do? Make devices correct, this KX stage is a showcase for their business like a concept car for an automobile manufacture. The design makes it easy to spread and share the event. It is designed to go viral. That is baked in. It was built to feed social media. You tie in Instagram culture of over 1 billion accounts as I write this on 5/27/20 and you can see where this is going. A study came out 10/13/19 that said ¾'s of listeners (74%) confirmed they are more likely to listen to an album in its entirety following an artist performance. Another 32% said they listen ahead of the show to familiarize themselves. You can now see very powerful trends and behaviors here and apply them to your lifestyle and or business.

I view the phone as a part of the person now, an extension of themselves especially for the generation 35 and below. The phone has a camera, recorder, webcam etc. It is like I have said a P.E.D - Personal entertainment device and I will now add to this a "personal escapism device". That device is more addictive than any drug. You add gambling being legalized, marijuana being mainstreamed and on the road to legalization in America, the big pill culture led by the AMA who adds to the legal drugs being prescribed, energy drinks, coffee drinks and of course the old standby sugar we have one big "GYNORMOUS" ADDICTION ECONOMY that feeds one another going forward.

Now let's consider the iPhone pro series, which now allows anyone to shoot professional work that 10 years ago was not possible without the budget. Everything is all baked in. Shooting vertically and producing vertical content is now a done deal. I grew up horizontal, these kids are growing up vertical. I am way behind on this on a personal level. I understand it intellectually but must incorporate in my designs. I WOULD SAY IT IS IN MY BEST INTEREST TO SHOOT BASED ON THE SMART PHONE ESPECIALLY BEING PART OF THE MUSIC BUSINESS. 63% of the searches are mobile. I have wake up don't I.

In closing, in June 2017 when Katy Perry promoted her new album during a 4 day You Tube live stream that amassed 49 million views, I saw that the game had changed! She is one of the biggest artists on the planet and she exposed herself in a big brother style house for 4 days. She shared herself to her base. You can now look back and say she was ahead of this by 3 years before the pandemic. At her level she didn't have to do something like that, now we can say she saw the future in hindsight.

Addendum: Super group BTS did the largest pay per view concert that reached 756,000 concurrent people in June 2020. That is now a reality for a business model.

OBSERVATION TWENTY

The rise of the immersive media economy

Music will be a driver in this economy, with 5G making its global introduction during the corona pandemic the stage is set for the next wave! In surfing you should ride the wave, 5G will allow the enhanced altering experiences through devices. Music and gaming will be my focus, so please figure out yours.

The consumption economy will be exploding exponentially, so it behooves all of us to enhance our skill sets for this coming opportunity that is already here! VR will be emancipated via 5G which will allow people to do things with a device that will allow the consumer to be very present from a distance. The whole concept of proximity is being challenged. All of the Star Wars and Star Trek sci fi will be coming to life. The corona pandemic has sped this trend. There will be new platforms/services that will roll out with the wide adoption of 5G., this will allow I feel a massive shift in how the next generation meet up to attend social events.

THE MAINSTREAMING OF WHAT IS CALLED "DIGITAL HUMAN STREAMING TECHNOLOGY" WILL BE FLOODING THE WORLD. Please deep dive into that tech you need to know about it. What I call the "matrix economy" will be leading the way. By writing this I realized I have all of the parts scattered about, I need to put it all together as I finalize writing this narrative. My design is baked for the future.

The big part of the "matrix economy" for me is gaming. The leader at the moment is Epic Games Fortnite. I want to state, I have never played video games and will probably never play. However, I am fascinated by the video game ecosystem which is the key component to my future. The gamification of media/content is a trend I have been studying since 2018 and really hit me when DJ Marshmello and Fortnite partnered on their first concert Feb 2019. We now just experienced the Travis Scott concert experience during the pandemic April 2020. These are called "defining moments", as the great basketball coach/executive Pat Riley in many interviews during the playoffs and NBA finals interviews over the years has called these types of situations.

During the quarantine games have really ratcheted upwardly in usage. These games are played on mobile devices. People will sit with games for the whole day, especially the 12-25-year-old demo. I have witnessed this with my own eyes and did my own focus groups. With no time limits to free time during the pandemic, games exploded in general populace. Fortnite has become an industry on to itself. As of this writing on 5/27/20 Fortnite is played by 40% of kids 10-17 every week and 250 million players worldwide. Fortnite is also similar to a tv network now if not bigger because of the astounding numbers that it possesses. An example of this, the tentpole movie Tenet was advertised during the pandemic while theatres are closed. The movie Tenet which is the first big movie to be scheduled to open theatres in July 2020, a big ad campaign was executed showing just how critical Fortnite has become. Post script the theatres didn't open.

Now back to the "concert experience" by Travis Scott merchandise was debuted to sell during this record breaking event. 27.7 million concurrent players were the final numbers. By 2022 gaming is projected to be a 196-billion-dollar business. It dwarfs film and music already! Here are some numbers to chew on:

- 5 of the top 10 channels on You Tube in 2019 were connected to gaming.
- 1.2 billion tweets about video games
- Facebook launched a gaming app 2020.
- Twitch is based on live streaming games and now as I finish this narrative marrying with music which will fuel this immersive economy further.

I have several treatment ideas for a livestream show to display my media and content in 2021 so stay tuned.

I have designed and conceived my first mobile game which I started in October 2019 in a why not moment. The name of the game is #PULLOVAHHUNNY, which will display a different spin on dating. It was an incredible learning experience for me to go through and has definitely altered by immediate future. It has opened my eyes to exponential opportunities in the future that I am excited to explore. I could not have imagined doing this even a year ago, as I compose this final draft 8/10/20. I decided to go all in, the reason I mention this is to show what I am writing here is real and not a theory. Please go back to the forewarned in the beginning of the narrative when I discussed intra class opportunities. Reread that part now because it all becomes real.

Going forward I see virtual concerts will be a super-premium experience of intimate sessions for real fans of a brand/artist. The main character in "Pullovah Hunny" is based on a digital brand I am developing to build into its own constantly evolving storyline. Avatars will be an ever-increasing avenue to build digital based stories. Remember I mentioned digital streaming technology, I am creating my own. So please stay tuned. It starts with my own D.I.Y mobile game.

All content/media is to bring you into someone's world and to keep them there, so you can "move the needle". This will give anyone an opportunity to build a franchise or develop a compelling film or series. The thirst for credible I.P and top talent who can produce/develop will be done globally now. You have to open your mind to such a level of opportunity that awaits. You have private equity searching for this type of I.P

Final thoughts here, with the advent of 5G the fan will be able to join the act on the stage or go back stage with the growth of this technology. Headphones/your phone maybe able to mix the sound better to your individual liking, becoming the sound engineer. The individuals growing up with Instagram now see themselves as a celebrity, I won't say a star because a star is a process not a moment. Passivity is now a dead idea at concerts or experiences. For those types the music maybe a byproduct of the whole experience. I have tried to fit the most critical things here for people to really dive into on their own, I hope they take the time to do that.

OBSERVATION TWENTY-ONE

We are all bakers now

Everyone going forward will need to think like a bakery! You will have to think about all of your ingredients into what you are publishing. My favorite baker is Lord's in Brooklyn, Ny by Brooklyn College. Just thinking about Lord's takes me back to being ten years old. The reason why I am bringing this up is because one of my favorites is the fudge drop or the Chinese cookie. A lot of stores and other bakeries carry that cookie, it looks the same but the ingredients are totally different which alters the taste and the overall experience which leads to disappointment. That is the "tricknology" involved, because looks are very deceiving.

How you bake and develop your content will differentiate the taste of your media/content, this will impact how people react to it. Make sure you have baked in all of your key ingredients. When you are developing your media/content.

Here I will discuss who I look to for signals in the corporate world. I monitor Apple and Disney. These two mega corps are the deans of mixing and matching media/images to a moment that becomes a frozen moment in time. Those two companies display the critical details if you take the time to notice. I still go about my business based on my ideas and positioning but use Apple/Disney as a weather vane.

The future I feel in the post corona economy, all of us as advertisers will have the same options available in principle. Either spend your money on advertising on or in other people's media, or you build your own branded content and then invest heavily to get eyeballs on what you are publishing. IT IS JUST THAT SIMPLE. I have chosen to do my own internal production versus spending with outside vendors. I was already doing this because of being in the independent music game for so long where you have no choice but to create and invest in your own vision. You have to believe in yourself always. In that world you never have enough resources but your belief will get you places you couldn't have imagined just by doing.

Apple TV was started on this idea; I know that Apple is an almost two trillion-dollar company that can place its products throughout the media they produce and can access any resource that is available, I am just attempting to show you we are all in the same business. Disney Plus is the same but different because they already have media that goes back over 90 years. That is the overarching message, BUILD INTERNALLY. I am using all of my "INTANGIBLE ASSETS" which in the post corona economy will be very tangible depending on how I use them. I am using my network of thousands of people and more importantly my experiences developing my music career from scratch. You don't realize what you have actually done until you get a chance to stare at the wall and reflect.

I have collected a lot of data and information. I have utilized social media from its genesis. I have worked with various startups over the years. That is how I procured Sony distribution. The intelligence network I have developed from doing so much travelling in a very granular fashion is baked in. We covered over 60 cities in North America and Canada, lived in London for three-year period that allowed us to cover the U.K and Ireland several times over and over. We also travelled to Germany and Russia. That is why I say music is an amazing thing. It is nothing like breathing the air in another continent! This is what the old music industry leaves you with. How do you put a dollar figure on that? You really can't until you do something with all of these soft assets or skill sets which is what I will do in the immediate future. Many of the tech wonks if you dig into their background, they are what I call "frustrated musicians", Daniel Elk of Spotify is one of them I believe.

THE 2020"S WILL BE THE AGE OF THE CO_SIGN OF YOURSELF!!! This is why you must become a baker! Everything you do will have to be baked in by you. This will save marketing cost and more importantly put your unique vision out to the world, that will have you ahead of others. Most of us possess limited dollars. In the old world it was called product placement. In your face advertising doesn't work for me. I must get something back tangible! As a baker you can place all of your messages/work throughout your media/content. Do your own DeFacto exhibition to your captive audience.

Now I am going to discuss Drake the rapper/lyricist/entertainer/investor as a point-blank example. During the pandemic Drake released a song named the TOOSIE SLIDE. This song was custom fitted for the Tik Tok platform with a dance already embedded in the lyrics. Tik Tok has made a cultural statement via the dance challenge. Drake baked the song perfectly. He reached out to top dance influencers and sent the song to them, so they would set up the actual dance to it. It would be already baked in. It was a simple dance that anyone could do and not feel intimidated. The eased baked in. The dance influencers uploaded snippets to the site to start the tsunami prior to the official release. Drake further communicated with them while making the song. Once he saw the dance Drake named the song after dancers. THAT WAS GENIUS, because who is not going promote themselves. The hook of the song gives directions on how to do the dance. THE KEY PART OF THE DANCE SECTION CLOCKS IN AT 15 SECONDS WHICH TELLS YOU IT WAS TOTALLY CONCEIVED FOR THE TIK TOK PLATFORM WHICH IS THE RELEVANT PLATFORM OVER THE LAST 18 MONTHS. It is also the most relevant which is the perfect double whammy.

In closing, the overarching message is how the most successful companies, brands, artist and creators are baking and catering. They are putting in the critical unique ingredients to get people involved which is what anyone will need to do going forward. Make sure you have all of the correct ingredients measured before you start baking your product/service/media/content. This will also be the most fun part of what you do. The idea of bringing something from nothing will be an amazing fulfilling moment. GET TO IT. BUT MOST IMPORTANT KNOW THAT YOU ARE PRIVILEGED EVEN TO HAVE AN OPPORTUNITY TO DO THIS.

OBSERVATION TWENTY-TWO

The 2020's and how it will be a whole other world.

THE FUTURE WILL BE BLACK AND BROWN. It will be the time for the cultures that have been considered backwards and to some still not considered human coming into their own. If you take the time to look at the map you have to see where the future will be in this business. A real transformation will be taking place in my eyes and the seeds have been planted. When I started in 2016 reevaluating my business design the music business didn't really exist anymore and I had to become a student of technology. I almost quit music because I was heartbroken and was listening to all of the press about the demise of music. The music business was going to be based on streaming from a sales model which curtailed revenue, I saw it would be impossible to survive. A funny thing happened along the way though, the technologist was basing their business on music but not paying the rights holders. I then took the time to take another look at things and where I was headed. To be honest I didn't see what I could do when I looked at this new economy. I had been sequestered in music and night life; I like to call this the land of illusion....lol.

I must have sat with 15 business consultants of all types at SCORE NYC. I like to call it my listening tour. I went to many entrepreneurial meet ups. The more *I* listened the more I saw technology had "Houdinied" the economy but my saving grace would be music and marketing. Those two would be the underbelly of this new economy, subjects I am well versed in. I saw that songs not music (intellectual property) would have value. I saw that everywhere that people were discussing storytelling, I said to myself who tells stories more than music people. I kept seeing boot strapping and I said to myself I live in the boot...lol. The next logical thought was why was I quitting or feeling down and out. Here was a huge opportunity to reboot and reinvent everything. I saw that technology was my future but from the culturally/economic/psychological/ philosophical angle. Once I did this, it brought me a clarity because I saw what the end game was and how I had to fit in.

I saw that what the western world called the 3rd world was my future and I do have a great potential and propensity to flourish. I had to start the long trail of repackaging, reinventing myself and business design around the clock because I was so far behind. I saw that the smart phone will be the key to the business design especially in the 3rd world. I looked into the whole ecosystem of the smart phone since 2016. I guess you could call me a fanatic because I actually have a strong dislike for them, due to the fact I have to stay hooked up to it.

The keys to all of these wonderful trends I saw will be power (energy), bandwidth, financial infrastructure and clean water. All we have to do is look at ourselves here in the west where we have consistent power, unlimited bandwidth, financial infrastructure and access to clean water to see what will take place over there. Those key things we take for granted daily. The areas of Southeast Asia, India and Africa in my eyes is the future. We are talking about 3.3 billion people estimated. If you include Latin America, we are discussing more than half the world. For the most part I am discussing the first three areas. It is so much to this story but I will make it concise here. It will be up to individuals reading here to follow up themselves.

Let me start: Why is Facebook along with big telecom companies (China Mobile, MTN, Global Connect Orange and Vodaphone) building the most advance subsea cable to serve the African continent and the middle eastern region, where nearly a billion people are offline or have inconsistent costly internet? Why is Facebook spending 5.7 billion dollars on the Jio platforms in India for just ten percent of the company? These two very important things took place at the height of the pandemic in May 2020. For me this was very crucial because it told me my theorem was correct. THE OLD TRICK OF FOLLOW THE MONEY! I am not saying that big corporations' plans are always correct, what I am saying is they get paid not to make mistakes and do the due diligence. It told me that I better recalibrate my future and speed up certain internal plans. Both investments are geared toward what people in certain think tanks call "THE RISING BILLION". Those billions of people will have to be viewed totally different to succeed in the post corona economic future.

Let's take a look, those smart mobile devices will allow those billions to be reached with our messages, your service and finally your product. For the most part this mobile communication is very cheap or free. Now these people will be able to be accessed by anyone also. They themselves can now be heard! That part will have massive consequences for us comfortable people in the western economies. In time self-empowerment will come especially from the youth culture! I said to someone the poorest people can now see our wealth. It is not a secret anymore or an imagination. At some point don't you think they will say, I want some of that and go about figuring out how to get it. PLEASE MEDITATE ON THIS BEFORE YOU GO FORWARD.

My future is aligned with those people. In my business of music and gaming these rising billion have become a viable economic market. They live on a few dollars' day at the moment but that will change very shortly. Universal records, the largest record company on the planet just started Def Jam Africa during the pandemic. They have also opened offices in South east Asia in the late 2019 early 2020. These aggregate investments tell me I need to move much faster and my direction is correct. If I follow the money then I will be ok. That the rising billion will have the growing ability to stream content via their mobile devices is a given in this equation. Why was Jack Dorsey the CEO of Twitter embedded in Nigeria (Lagos) for an extended period in late 2019 to early 2020? Please think about this for a moment.

In regards to streaming the numbers it is astounding think about. The massive youth culture located in all of those places, that are growing up comfortable with this technology. After communicating with young Africans and having watched from 2013 till now, how their voices are now heard mainstream in western culture via the afrobeat music culture it shows what will be coming next.

The microfinancing and the wireless communication are the opening volley. You can now collab with billions of people via the thing that is in your pocket! This communication technology disperses "cultural power". You better stop and think about it right now. We here in the west had a monopoly on cultural hegemony for so long we think it is our god given right for people to follow us here in the west. Even if we don't say it, we feel it, because so long we have set the tone. I WILL SAY HERE GOOD LUCK WITH THAT ATTITUDE IN THE FUTURE PRESENT.

Let me go back to Facebook for a brief moment! We are in the same business as they are! We are all in the traffic business, subscriber business and garnering followers to hopefully lead to sales and or viewership. THIS IS WHY I SAID THE HUNGER GAMES OF CONTENT. Facebook or any platform is about themselves because they have to consume the most precious resource every human has, which is time. I REPEAT WE ALL JUST HAVE 24 HOURS. This why I have always hated to go to sleep...lol.

I will continue dropping bombs here.... We are always on these devices. These devices via free platforms are constantly being filled with free content by us humans. It is constantly being refreshed by us. The platforms do not have to pay for this content and for the most part that is being uploaded 24/7. Everyone is chasing "famedom"! It is genius yet diabolical because it preys on the many human conditions. This is just a small tip of the sword! I hope you understand why FB is laying those cables now. The human populace is the product! Yes, all of us are just a product now!!! Stop here and meditate on that.

I must come back to the "rising billion" again. For myself as a media/content provider a billion is the new magic number for enormous success. In the old music industry, it was 1 million which is called platinum status. A billion subscribers are the number subscription businesses worldwide are hoping to reach, as of the last public number I saw in July 2020 was 341 million paid globally. Now I hope you can see the importance of what Facebook has done. I have to go back again, remember I mentioned fin tech or financial technology. Now I will fully connect the dots. The subject is vast and I feel anyone reading this should dig to find out more. Billions are still unbanked, credit cards do not exist for the rising billion, so I pose the question.... how do they pay for a subscription? There smart phone is where the bank is, as you can see, we keep going back to that device. PLEASE STOP AND LOOK AT YOUR PHONE NOW FOR A MOMENT.

The legal issues will have to be resolved. I am speaking from a music business perspective, which I have said is the underbelly of so much of this. The key for the digital music business future has to be resolved during this post corona economy globally. Corona virus shutdown has cost trillions in human gathering businesses worldwide, which has affected culture in unspeakable ways. MUSIC CAN" T SURVIVE ON STREAMING ALONE; this was exposed during the virus pandemic. The less than 1/2 a penny you get for a stream is essentially giving it away. Imagine how many times that less than ½ has to be split. This is why the billion is the new million in the digital world. The live event portion of the music game is where the big transactions are, that business is in a state of limbo now. During the pandemic musicians performed via live streaming but that for the most part has been free and doesn't provide a livable wage as of now. THE MUSIC RIGHTS SITUATION HAS TO BE RESOLVED GLOBALLY. That is where those billions come into play. This will allow two sustainable sources of revenue, publishing and live streaming.

We have to get people use to paying even a very small fee for a live stream performance by the average artist even if it the fans are not use to paying. For example, if 100,000 people globally would pay $4.99 to watch a performance that would be a $500,000 gross. It is all based on numbers. This is why that billion number is so important, 100,000 in a world of 7 billion online is a small number. Remember micro/macro, incremental/exponential. Just thinking about the African continent of 1.2 billion estimated, that 100,000 doesn't seem so large now.

In this on demand economy we live in live marketing is the only way to go. It allows a level of must see and gives you an upfront priority. As an independent music veteran, I know it will be our future meal ticket. The on-demand economy is based on short term conversion of the consumer in regards to the long-term brand consideration. You must consider the risk of churning on this on demand consumption world. The consumer controls your fate. You better be giving them what they need and want. Remember the hunger games and the ultimate resource of 24 hours exist daily for each of us.

The real key for the I.P of global rights 'holders is once the rising billions are tied into the system with the capability to pay the rights holders, we will see a whole sale metamorphous take place. Once China, India, Africa develops a culture of respecting the copyright, billions of dollars will be instantly created. Copyrights /trademarks are the buttress of the creative capital business and is not respected or understood in those cultures. IMAGINE WHEN WE GET THEM ONBOARD. This will change the bottom lines for the creative class around the world. This is a cultural and legal issue. The technology is in place for this behavior to be altered via education.

All of these devices in my eyes are retail stores, a place to earn money. Remember big picturism I spoke on earlier. This is the big picture for me in the 2020's, the corona pandemic has definitely sped this up. All of these ½ pennies will add up. To put it in perspective how much is 1 billion x .0005? It equals 5 million dollars. Again, this is just the tip of the iceberg.

During the corona pandemic imaginations were rewritten. I learned also that China's northeast is being called the new California for film and content by Alibaba, Baidu and Tencent companies, who are the heavy hitters in China. In Africa, there has always been Nollywood. The producers there know how to shoot on a shoestring; the true D.I.Y. India has the almighty Bollywood that has an incredible lineage.

In closing, as undiscovered cultural behaviors, sounds, art are introduced to the western world a changing of the guard will take place, which will shake our foundation here in the west. In the 2020's it is time to open our minds, so you will be ready, willing and able to do business during this time of exciting change and transition.

OBSERVATION TWENTY-THREE

Normal does not exist anymore

This observation is one I have always felt. The idea of normal in this post corona period for me is to realize normal has to be erased from my personal narrative and business design!! I also feel to live in the 2020's normal will be a very fluid concept. It will always be a moving target now and will be in a constant disruption. I have been really thinking about normal and how it has kept me in a box. It allowed fear and lack of timely confidence in what I was doing in the moment to hold me back. It has stopped who I want to be in my life trying to be normal. Appeasing those around me because what I may have thought would be too far out for them. That has always made me feel squeezed! Trying to be normal was one the worse mistakes throughout my life. Stifling ideas constantly because I didn't feel I had a sounding board around me, so you spend your time over questioning yourself, which then freezes you and the opportunities go on by.

The confirmation bias that we all possess was killing me slowly. I am looking for someone that is open to the possibilities not just probabilities. I never found that sounding board. I know I am not the only one feeling that way. Instead we spend so much of life chasing normal, thinking that it will work out, to me now that is a very false statement. IF YOU HAVE IDEAS AND VISIONS YOU WILL BE OUT OF SYNC WITH THE MAJORITY OF INDIVIDUALS.

The corona period and now the George Floyd induced protests along with all of the technological trends that are formulating, normal will be constantly uprooted! I am now stating normal will be changing much more violently. There is no time to worry about being normal anymore! I have now coined #NORMALDOESNOTPAY hashtag. Normal used to be going to the club and dancing closely with a total stranger. As I write, that is considered a life-threatening idea. There is no more time to be worrying about being normal or fit in a box somewhere. THAT IS INDUSTRIAL AGE THINKING! On a personal level, I was not that person seeking normal. I see the world from a very wide vision. As a child, I looked at the globe and said I want to walk every inch of it. Material things were never important to me, I just wanted to live and experience the globe that we live on.

As a teenager, I looked at the quote un quote normal life and I knew I didn't want to do that. As a black kid in America all you are told was limits and being cautious in your socially acceptable normal. Go to school, get a job and work your whole life and retire. When I looked at the normal around me, I knew it was not for me, and I came from a decent neighborhood! I can look back now and realize I have been trying to avoid normal my whole life. I feel at this point for me, it makes the most sense to uninstall normal from my personal algorithm. It is a stifling idea to me. I know there are a lot of people battling this idea of normal with me and I hope they join me.... lol.

When you look at the world, all of the things we use were not normal! The telephone, the airplane, the refrigerator, the list can go on and on, they were not normal. Let's look at the definition of normal:

Conforming to a type, standard, or regular pattern. According with, constituting, or not deviating from a norm, rule or principle.

I realize to do what I want to do; I MUST UNINSTALL NORMAL. If you look at history normal doesn't really exist, control and oppression does. Normal is something imprinted upon us. As we come into adulthood normal is a "progression killer". As we move along normal is something that must be questioned by young adults especially if you do not have a trust fund. Normal takes away choices and options from us.

I realize now that nothing in the 2020's will be normal. The whole idea of normal has been shredded. The whole idea of normal is a pre digital lifestyle based on the industrial age. I will state here now, If I am truly living digital and following what I have written here, normal has nothing to do with it. PLEASE STOP HERE AND MEDITATE ON THAT STATEMENT.

When you are always asking questions, you are threatening normal! Normal does not like to be threatened. I totally realize going forward, I have to constantly threaten normal. It will be my job to threaten normal on a daily basis. I am on my way to finally creating my own lane as a #observationtheorist. I will not call myself a futurist. All what I have done here is to observe and connect the many pieces of the "jigsaw puzzle" that are placed in front of us on a daily basis. No school or rules! It all is how each individual takes their unique lifestyle, lens to the world and decipher what is in front of them. I have no PHD, Master's degree or a direct lane to the road I am embarking on. I am creating my own lane in this post corona economy. I thank you for giving me an opportunity to bring this to life in front of the world. For me, this is about inspiring people to go create opportunities. As of this day of 8/11/20 at 12:37pm NORMAL HAS BEEN UNINSTALLED FROM MY PERSONAL ALGORITHM.

OBSERVATION TWENTY-FOUR

Cultural posturing and cultural resonance = Bonus material

6/8/20 12:13pm – I am observing so much with the daily protest about George Floyd. There are way too many things to discuss here, but I had to say something here that correlates to the narrative of what we are doing here. This paragraph is very critical to what we are doing and it may make some people uncomfortable. But since we have uninstalled normal being comfortable is something that needs to be questioned also.

In 2020 authenticity and what poses as reality are being driven by much posturing, using snap imagery that can exponentially travel. The NFL is one organization I will bring up here and discuss. Roger Goodell is the face of ownership as the commissioner, made an abrupt U turn on the kneeling issue that blackballed Colin Kaepernick since the year of 2017. How can the NFL say they didn't know? They were not aware of the problem! One of their own, who played in the Super Bowl 2013, who actually explained why he was doing the kneeling eloquently to the public, was blackballed, ostracized, lost his job and was never given a proper chance to have a dialogue. The NFL never made an attempt to have a dialogue, the NFL just did the old school remove the problem. However, in a social media age, the old school doesn't work anymore. Fast forward three years later due to the visual murder of George Floyd at the hands of the police, the NFL is now listening! After nationwide protest for ten days the NFL is listening! Who are we kidding!!!!

The ownership threatened their majority African American work force (players) to not follow Mr. Kaepernick and now you are listening. The NFL could have led on this issue but they waited to the last minute with nationwide unrest everywhere and the PR pressure growing for them to speak up. THAT WAS NOTHING BUT POSTURING! NOTHING AUTHENTIC. On a professional but more on a personal level it was a travesty of human inaction! The greater travesty is that the NFL will be given a pass! It won't even be a footnote in history, along with all of all of the other lost footnotes of history, that is why I am mentioning it here. I love the NFL like most, but I can't give them a pass because from a marketing perspective it was all wrong as well. THE INFAMOUS DOUBLE WHAMMY.

Due to the digital dominance of our daily lives it is important for all of us as consumers to understand what posturing is and how it relates to your brand, but more importantly in your ultimate job on this planet as a human being. Let's look at the definition:

Behavior that is intended to impress and mislead.

Next up is being culturally resonant and being mindful of the current anxieties. I just witnessed the NFL do this also. Mr. Goodell spoke the language of now, which is racism, social justice and police brutality especially to their workforce and the African American consumers in the USA. In history there is a treasure trove of historical incidences that this fake behavior has been repeatedly displayed. The NFL has just spoke the language of now! You want to be part of the hottest trends. Show that your brand is part of the solution not the problem. Generation Z, who in the 2020's will be the dominant consumer group is big on this cultural resonance. You must be aware of this as you move forward in all you do.

I have decided to share a personal story here after careful thought and deliberation. I have applied those principles to the George Floyd tragedy because as an African American male who has worn the uniform for this country it hits home very hard.

At times in your daily life you have to walk around defensively in your posture as an African American. I battle it daily. You can't extinguish it from your personal algorithm a hundred percent. One of the most profound moments in my life happened outside of America. It was when I was in London at a meeting with music and creative people. I ended up at an old warehouse building in east London and the folks were discussing being free and having liberty. For the record, the place was a bomb shelter in WWII when Hitler was dropping major bombs on London trying to break the spirit of the people. I happen to be the only black person; it shouldn't matter but coming from USA it is something that is very present in your mind. The most important thing was I was the only American in the room.

For the first hour I didn't speak, however when I opened my mouth the whole room focused on me. They asked where I was from.... am I from the states? I said no, I said I am from Brooklyn....some laughed and some had a quizzical look on their face so I explained. I said America happens outside of New York City. They all wanted to come to the states based on the ideals in America of liberty, freedom and justice. I then said America has many problems! I said as a black man living in America, I have issues and are viewed as a second class citizen or not seen as a human being. They could not believe what I was saying to them. We are talking 19 people. The defining moment was calling myself black but not American. I defended that premise and repeated three times in a back and forth with many in the room who were from eastern Europe, New Zealand, Australia and Switzerland. They were saying no you are American.... I said I am black...they said your American....i said no I am black...they said no your American... I finally stopped and thought in that moment, I said to myself look what America has done to me. In order to bring an end to the back and forth I made a joke of it by saying It is a shame I have to fly six hours to be American because when I fly back seven hours and land at JFK airport, I become black again. In that moment I left all of the "black baggage" that is institutionally laid on all black people in America in my rear view mirror. The more compelling thing and shameful, is that I had to experience this outside of America. I am forever thankful I had that moment because it has bought me so much clarity in my life.

The concept/idea of America is an amazing marketing campaign. The constitution is an amazing document. All I can do is hope years down the road that all of the posturing and cultural resonance that America has done won't be needed anymore. I hope that you now understand the importance of these two things to your brand and you have aha moment. Let's hope for a better future.

OBSERVATION TWENTY-FIVE

AI and intellectual property

While doing my daily due diligence I came across an article by Bas Grasmeyer posted on 12/9/2019. For me it was a frightening article if you view music as an art form and not a commodified widget. My initial business plan is based on the 1998 DMCA which is totally antiquated yet still on the books. As an independent record label, I didn't realize I have been literally on the front line of this subject but from a different context. Every single big tech media company has used this law to create their trillion-dollar businesses. No one wants to discuss this because it is really a dirty crime that uses obfuscation. I am not here to go deep into that here but it needs to be mentioned due to the context.

The subject of "Authorless music" is the end game of the big tech companies. Meaning no copyright infringement cases. This takes out the human component. NO rightsholders to deal with. That is a wonderful thing if you are not a creator of music. There would be no more take down notices, no lawsuits and you could in theory just have a wild west of content being used. The "digerati elite" argues that those things above holds up the real capacity of the open source system because it stops the usage of music and films etc. As I said above these big tech companies just ripped the IP for many years.

Google through its lobbyist would wish to do away with the copyright or water it down so much that it is a Poodle instead of a Rottweiler. I am not picking on Google, just touching upon the digerati thought here and who epitomizes this better than Google.

Artificial Intelligence will explode a trend called "utilitarian music! I will say here that you already see this via the playlist encroaching so much on the artist album. The playlist and the album are similar yet so different. The playlist is commodified and the artist album is personal, storytelling and a work of art from an individual. Remember a human is a complex creature. AI is not. The human has to sleep, the AI does not. Human is incremental, the AI has everything in its favor to be exponential. AI will be trained by the algorithm, by music of thousands of artists not one specific artist. The underlying business proposition is there will be no cost, no rights issue. You could do whatever you wanted with the music. No need to track down a rights owner to pay them or some organization. That sounds so wonderful to people in the tech space who won't reveal their algorithm but want you to give away your sweat and toil.

This AI music will increase songs in theory to a "gazillion" a year. I will now say the other side of the equation. There will be less works of art. Less emotion with this robot music. I want you now to apply this idea above to your profession, business and your life. You better give it your deepest of thoughts because normal does not exist and disruption is the new normal. This definitely is in all of our futures. You can try to dodge this line of thought all you want but it is coming for you. You better be thinking when will my industry or my job be a disruption casualty because normal is continually being reevaluated. I recommend you start living digital even if you don't want to.

This observation is embedded in the whole design of the 2020's. This decade will be a compelling/challenging yet a very fruitful time if you adjust your lens to the world. The AI will impact our lifestyle immensely and this subject must be tackled by each forward-thinking individual.

OBSERVATION TWENTY-SIX

The Gift Wrap

Going through the mental battles, the constant reevaluations, the who I think I am, I have come to a conclusion of what has been my biggest issues. The biggest issues are myself and how I view the world. The biggest project, which I see will be an ongoing one of uninstalling the many different types of fears that encapsulate so much in my (our) mental psyche. The unrelated fears that we all build in our minds, that the bulk of the time if you reflect on our life after all is said and done, those fears didn't materialize. They were just in your mind based on ill fitted perceptions and visions that are designed to hold you in one place. Once you fully understand your own human condition, you will eventually start to see that you have wasted so much time and opportunities due to these fears. I will say you have to look at these fears when they approach you as an obstacle as part of an obstacle course. What do you do on an obstacle course? You go around them. Fears are convenient roadblocks we use at times in our lives to justify holding ourselves back based on quote unquote logical illogical things or events.

I have touched upon the negative fuel we gas ourselves with especially through the media and our education system. My focus here was media but the education system is actually more liable in my eyes. I mention it here to open that door for people to walk through on their own. It is not my place here. These fears take up our precious resource, by now I hope you know it is time! By looking at things I came up with I had to uninstall the idea of comfort and being comfortable yet still going down that worm hole of deeper frustration. How many of you here understand that? In case you don't, staying in these negative fuel situations for over extended periods of your life will burn your most precious commodity.

The thing about all of this is, I realize it is no school for this stuff because it is you as an individual that has to decide what you do. Also, each individual has a unique experience. That is what makes this so special. It is about what you decide to do with all you possess. No rules! It is all in how you decipher and implement. For me it all boils down to the U in unique. All of us have different lives and have walked different roads. IT IS ONE BIG INTANGIBLE.

I see massive opportunities because of being an #digitalcitizen, opportunity will constantly unfold in front of me. My job is to see them. When I mention digital citizenship, it is not about the physical technology but more of the human side of it. You can purchase technology but that doesn't mean you are #livingdigital or on your way to digital citizenship. Living digital is the opposite of how we are wired. The human condition dictates routine, familiarity that leads to simplicity, which is great in the moment but can stunt your growth. The construct of that antiquated term failure is positive fuel now for you. Embrace those lessons. The secret is to move away from it and go to the next stage with the experiences learned without dwelling!

I hope you can see the evolution through the pages and the growth right before your eyes. It has been a gestation of period of 4 years of grinding every day. The corona pandemic has totally changed how artistic types create, but more importantly everyone is looking at their financial survival. This is one of those moments when everyone is at a fork in the road and have to make concrete/forward thinking decisions. As I said, we all now are in the music business. Everyone is a "professional busker" now. I remember my days in London of hanging out with this busker on Sundays sipping tea to stay warm in Leicester Square in London. Priceless experience sitting out there freezing watching him do his craft and making the tea runs. Shout out to my main man Paul! I could not have imagined, but that is the whole point.... imagining, something that I must do again to make it in these 2020's.

The industrial life is over and we are in the digital life now. There will be many hurdles and growing pains going through this change. For those who embrace what I have said here, I believe you will come out the other side of this fine and dandy.

I hope you see that this is a global phenomenon not localized, meaning there is very little wiggle room. The only way to protect yourself and your future is to prepare and alter yourself. THE HARDEST PART WILL BE OURSELVES, due to the human condition. Please take the time to dive into yourself and change that algorithm to benefit your future. That is what Facebook, Google and Amazon do periodically. GET TO CHANGING.

Since we are humans most of the growth will be incremental not exponential. It will be I hope a fascinating journey similar to my own. Create a journal so you can keep track of your growth. TAKE ALL OF THE SHACKLES FROM YOUR PAST OFF. You have to remind yourself of what it was like to go to that first day of Kindergarten. See yourself as a blank chalk board. Please remember the innate beauty of that chalkboard.... you can erase!!! Please apply to your future development.

To close, I have a compelling quote from an unknown source.

We always tend to think of history as somehow predetermined. Of course, the Romans won, but so often great twists of history turn on a few decisions, a single battle, an unexpected invention, a visionary or fanatic's charisma.

I hope all of you reading take this to heart. I am saying here you can make a defining moment in your own life. You have a chance to make the twist in your favor. Good luck, let's go get it. Do not just be a bystander in your own life.

OBSERVATION TWENTY-SEVEN

The only way is forward

We will have to learn to flourish in the unknown. That will be our secret sauce to future success. We now live in the age of the "casino of content"! This will also give the ordinary people an unprecedented opportunity to have success that in the past needed the wealthy or the billion-dollar corporation. The ordinary will also be coming of age with a voice that can be heard. THE QUESTION IS WILL IT BE HEARD ABOVE THE CACOPHONY OF CONTENT. We have just witnessed this with the George Floyd tragedy.

Conceiving this narrative has allowed me to realize without a doubt I have to totally embrace the digital perspective to have a prosperous decade. It has been a four-year journey for me, with the last 3 years being completely immersive. I feel have arrived to what I call a #DIGITALCITIZEN now, yet maintain my analog upbringing. I hopefully will try to maintain the best of both.

Marketing is what will get all of us ahead of others in this tsunami of content that will be heading our way. I am just starting to comprehend and put this jigsaw puzzle that the digerati have given us to full use. Please remember: TRUTH IS LEARNED! The "digerati" class have done the greatest "sleight of hand" to the masses around the world. THE HUMAN HAS BECOME THE PRODUCT. Look at yourself as a product every time you are on a social media site. The 2020's will bring all of these trends together that was discussed here to completely transform the economy and people's lifestyle. You better decide what part of the global game that is being played on us you will be a part of. To be more blunt WHAT SIDE OF THE TABLE YOU WILL BE ON.

All of your campaigns, projects and or businesses will have to give value or something of substance to another human being. The intangible here is value and whatever that means to another person. This is why I said you better understand culture. In the past it was just enough to entertain but now it is so much more I feel. How you view the world, will be crucial to your future success.

Stability has been replaced by ever increasing disruption. The mass market is being replaced by the micro market and by much smaller payment structure. We must all figure out in what micro space you/your business will land in. Altruism will be a critical component of I call #memarketing. Altruism apparently activates the same part of the brain as food and sex. Those two things are a large part of what a human being is based on. You better be asking how does your campaign impact the audience! The main question will be, is it something they will be proud to share or be a part of. THAT IS THE WHOLE POINT OF YOUR CAMPAIGN, AS WE FAST TRACK INTO A GROWING COLLABORATIVE CONSUMPTION ECONOMY. Will it allow reciprocation? That is why Tik Tok and Instagram work so well.

Make sure your reputation stands for something distinctive. It must breed that BIG TRUST in the digital space because it is through a screen and not physical. The probability of getting a second chance in the digital diaspora is very low.

The hormone Oxytocin is released in the brain, when you part of a group. That key hormone promotes feelings of love, bonding and well-being. This is why it is crucial to keep your reputation high online, which will gravitate people to you.

Every down turn in the economy has made the network stronger at every turn. This corona pandemic is no different. Once the human gets accustomed to new behaviors it is hard to go back. What was once a luxury for the elite of society becomes regular. The omnipresent trickle-down effect of technologies has happened during this corona pandemic. Each economic setback creates an allege convenience as it is sold to the public to open it to wide spread adoption. We have just witnessed this during the pandemic.

The key will be WHAT WILL YOUR MIND ALLOW YOU TO DO? PLEASE MEDITATE ON THAT.

Living digital makes everything a work in progress. That is something you must dedicate yourself to understanding. I will remind you here of "continuous integration", please go back and look at it.

Lazy is dead in the fast-changing future – Warren Whitlock

The digital world is not a wait and see world! The people who wait and see will be behind and not heard. Remember you must be an actor.

I am going to close with this statement from an unknown source because it sums up what we are doing here in the 2020's:

WHEN YOU ARE TRAVELLING AHEAD OF THE CURVE IT IS SILLY TO IMAGINE THE ROAD WILL BE SMOOTH, STRAIGHT AND FLAT, IT IS CLIFFS AND BUMPS, YOU ARE IN THE VOID, AHEAD OF THE CURVE....AHEAD OF WHAT IS BEHIND, AHEAD OF THE CURVE WEATHER IS PRETTY LOUSY. THE BLESSING IN THIS WILL BE WORKING IN THAT MESS WILL ALLOW YOU TO FIND A NEW PATH.

OBSERVATION TWENTY-EIGHT

My Truth

The keys to the jigsaw puzzle are to look at all of this from a historical systems/ideas and culture perspective. From the global perspective it has been always the patricians versus the proletariat. This has been going on since written history commenced. Let's look at the definition of those two terms:

Patrician – Aristocrat or nobleman. Someone belonging to or related to a royal, noble or wealthy family.

Proletariat – workers or working-class people, regarded collectively (often used with reference to Marxism). The lowest class of citizens in ancient Rome.

Take a look at the American revolution, French revolution and Russian revolution to see through the haze of history. I will focus very briefly on the American system. The system is based on the individual and for the government to remain in the background not to have a heavy hand in the citizens life.

I am an economic history guy. I must mention these two-key characters that have a very quiet yet overwhelming influence in our life daily. They are Adam Smith and Karl Marx.

Adam Smith – Is considered the first theorist of what we commonly refer to as capitalism.

Karl Marx – Most modern forms of communism/socialism is grounded at least nominally in Marxism, a theory and method conceived by Karl Marx during the 19th century.

Most of us do not comprehend that most of the debates of the modern time in politics center around what these two guys postulated. It would be in the best interest to anyone reading to look at these two if you have not done prior. Once you understand these two then you will be able to see where you fit in. As an American, the document the constitution is something that those reading here should take a deep dive into. Once you do that then you will need to take a look at the magna carta. Once you start to really dive deep into that period you start to see what was really the theme of most debates you see in the news in modern history. The key to all of this is for you as an individual to see "what side of the table you are sitting on". Your future really depends on this. It is imperative you take the time on this. You can't afford to react emotionally to what are overarching systems being thrown at you. Due to your limited understanding of these systems you act emotionally instead of intellectually based on sound principles.

Our past 160 years we have been consuming technological advances that have made our lives much better, I will be the first to say it. The flip side of this; we have become beholden to the technology.

One of the great liabilities of life is that all too many people find themselves living amid a great period of social change, and yet they fail to develop the new attitudes, the mental responses, that the new situation demands. They end up sleeping through revolution. MLK a week before his assassination.

Based on the MLK quote I will state how two professions have been totally redefined due to the digital space. Being a director or producer doesn't mean what it used to mean twenty years ago. It means totally something different in my eyes. Due to all of the technological advances, we are all creating on our own. Everyone is director/producer of their own content now from their home. What does a book publisher mean now? I am publishing this narrative myself. Does this mean I am Random House? Many other titles and professions are being redefined and don't mean what they use to mean.

The human is now a liability/expense. What happens when you are seen as an expense? You can get cut abruptly. The machine/robot/AI is seen as an asset. The digerati see the masses of humans as just lab rats for their algorithm and for "data servitude". The next wave of the "anti human" campaign commences during this corona pandemic. The future in the 2020's is really about how to innovate the machines at the expense of the human. It is only about machine automation not for human betterment. However, it will be depicted to us as better for us. That is a yes and no. It depends on what side of the table you are sitting on. It is in your best interest to understand the deeper process here. The public globally has voluntarily (although unknowingly) turned over to Google and Facebook far more personal information than the government will ever have.

I want you to fully understand that we are all in "DATA SERVITUDE" now. We are all an "INDENTURED DATA SERVANT". Please put that on your resume. The technologist aka "THE DIGERATI" have created a new unpaid position for us all. I think it is quite genius. They have a global employment force that works for them unknowingly. The digerati have used the human condition against us. The Robber Barons of the industrial age and the Mafia have nothing on these guys. The digerati have the global masses giving their platforms free content 24 hours a day and now have us paying to advertise.

I needed something to finally say goodbye here that is not based on technology. I found this quote in a book of quips and quotes, the quote made me freeze frame because it defines my message here perfectly:

WHEN YOU ARE IN A HOLE STOP DIGGING. UKNOWN SOURCE

Living in an analog/industrial age mentality will have you in a hole, that you are digging yourself. I have stated we live in a world of systems that I hope you will investigate much deeper. I am making a personal plea to stop digging yourself into a deeper hole because you resist to understand or investigate the digital economy going forward and to start erasing the industrial one in your personal algorithm.

We will have to embrace the process of constantly becoming. We will all have to be a "RENAISSANCE PERSON". You will have to reboot yourself or you are digging yourself into a deeper hole. The government via politicians and bureaucrats who the populace has been trained to look to will not tell you what I am telling you here. I am someone who has learned the hard way. I have explained it here in a humanistic and personal way, not from a teacher to student or expert to layman. I have explained it in everyday language. I am from the school of K.I.S.S (keep it simple stupid). The Individuals in seats of power/control wish to keep things complicated.

I am throwing my last pitch here; it will be a Mariano Rivera cut fastball. I am a Yankee fan. I truly miss him. The most prosperous business on the planet is #IGNORANCE. I hope here I have curtailed the profit of the biggest corporation on the planet, which I call Ignorance Inc. Cheers it has been a privilege. Peace and light to all.

THANK YOU

I would like to thank the main library in Jersey City for being my "incubation center" for my transition to "digital citizenship". I had the time to just let my mind wander and put together this global jigsaw puzzle. It was my escape hatch during the most frustrating period in my life. The library also purchased my first book Live Digital or Be Irrelevant and put me in their annual book fair. It allowed me to see that I could make this my future. I will be from this point on a writer/speaker/consultant/lifestyle maven from here on out. I am taking the plunge fully. That was an incredible experience for me and I feel privileged to have had that opportunity. Big love to the Grove street Starbucks for being my evening escape hatch. The crew of people I met there are spectacular. It was eye opening for me to meet such a diverse group of people in pursuit of their personal goals. Shout out to Kesha #teach. I watched her grind out an online master's degree over a lot of coffee. I saw the sacrifice. Aaliyah who is always on that super grind. She is an amazing business consultant who has an on the ground real opinion about how business works on the granular level. A big high five to former Starbucks crew CEO Joel out in LA. Good luck with your play and podcast. Thanks for the edit on "I am a statistic article" in the Jersey City Journal. Very special shout out to Vizi Henriquez aka Gift for allowing me to see things through the eyes of a 9-10-year-old in this time of exponential growth. You were my Tik Tok and Fortnite consultant this spring/summer of 2020. It allowed me to unlock so many roadblocks mentally. Much love to my former colleagues Carol, Dwayne and Tera at Prudential Center in Newark, I spent a lot of hours in that pantry formulating my maiden mobile game #PULLOVAHHUNNY. It was a pleasure to serve there with you. Shout out to Dr. Holness for his expertise on viruses during the corona pandemic. Someone with all of that knowledge should be making policy because he believes in the science and not the politics. We are still going to win. I have known Dr. Holness since I was 8 years old. Shoutout to Stephanie aka Solitaire for her spiritual clairvoyance during the pandemic. She possesses such a warm soul and spirit. As I tell her, can't wait till she leaves her cocoon. Major saving grace to Kevin Mcneill for the "suicide loans" and understanding during this elongated transition period. Shout to Ahmed and Thanuja Smith-ford for the home cook Sunday meals and a place to decompress. Shout out to Dr. Smith-Ford for assisting me with the early conception of the cover over the phone and much success with your return to the music business. He is a holistic doctor which was comforting in this corona environment of information fraud. Big ups to Terry P as he embarks on new beginnings. It is unbelievable what we started in a basement as kids hanging out turned out to be a business. This allowed the venerable Frank's in Fort Greene, Brooklyn on Fulton Street to live on for another generation. I tip my hat. Great conversation during the pandemic. Special shout to Gloria Jones for being a very understanding investor. I don't know if and how I will be able to give you back your hard-earned money. That is very bothersome to me but I plan to make it right. A shout out to Emi from my Barclay High team. Fist bump to Juan from Barclay High. Suites wasn't sweet all the time, but we did the dang thing. It has been an honor to reconnect with a child hood buddy Carl H. What a mind! An intellectual powerhouse. Very refreshing speak with you. Also, TRAEDONYA! aka "The Bride of New Funk Hipopera" the music is still magical. So much was left on the table and the last 8 years was a lost period. I won't go into details here. The investment that went into the music and developing your brand will be lost if nothing is done with it. It was 20 years nonstop flight in my life. We were indie before it was fashionable in music. I know we were ahead of the curve as I look back now. We never got to that one person who could have totally understood what we were doing. I see we were ten years to early. Remember TRAE'S ROADHOUSE. We Can't go back in time but we have time in the future to make this right, because right now it all wrong. Big shout to Serge and the Sullivan Room community for coming to my aid during the pandemic. That was an amazing thing to witness. We have to get the documentary done.

I owe "quarantine living" for allowing me to have the time to go through all of my possibilities without any friction from the outside world. It brought me back to seeing the world from one of abundance and positivity. It allowed me to write this narrative as a real writer. I just got up and knocked out pages and had the time to deliberate.

In closing, special thank you to my former intern Chelsea Frazer to take up the task of becoming my book editor. You taught me a lot the summer of 2019. Thank you for riding with me, though things were not completed I am still in hot pursuit. It is still very disappointing to me and wish a few things were different. At least I completed this narrative. Any time I can do anything for you in the future, please do not hesitate. August 12th 2020 8:07pm.... this is complete. This has been real privilege. I can't believe it is done. Ready to embark on a whole new lifestyle. Hooray! On the waterfront.

ACKNOWLEDGEMENTS

I want to thank intern Chelsea Frazer who spent the summer of 2019 with me working on all of the plans that I am introducing. Ms. Frazer is a budding music journalist/writer. She has decided to tackle the job of book editor. She has shown me the value of realizing that my experiences don't mean what they use to mean in my professional life. It is truly fascinating to watch her embark on her life, as I redesign and reinvent mine. This has been a very bumpy and tumultuous road while I am literally "figuring it out" on a daily basis. I found a business design that I feel can always be ready for change. I will be executing the rollout of this narrative Spring of 2021. Special thank you to the YMCA on west 63rd in Manhattan for being an incredible giving environment to finish this narrative in the style of Ernest Hemingway. I really felt like a writer from yesteryear working in that sparse environment. I went a week locked in a room to get this completed along with my mystery editor online. We grinded it out. Thank you so much for the uncredited role. Please reach me at https://akcidentalwriter.com if you wish to connect on a deeper level. I am available for consultations and speaking on this exciting innovative subject. The name of my final narrative for this trilogy on #humaninnovation is called Thinking Grey: A human innovative thought landscape for the post corona digital society. Stay tuned for that one late 2021 or early 2022. It has been a privilege to share this fluid construct with you. Thank you for your patronage.

www.ingramcontent.com/pod-product-compliance
Lightning Source LLC
Chambersburg PA
CBHW081414080526
44589CB00016B/2532